Printed in the United States of America
Erin Lawler Patterson 2017

ISBN: 978-1544282411

Erin Lawler Patterson
New Jersey
www.goodnesschick.com

Table of Contents

1 Thoughts From the Drug Lady 1
2 Being Presently Present 5
3 Laundry Cycles 9
4 Don't be a Stubby Candle 17
5 Haitian Perspective 26
6 R-E-S-P-E-CT 31
7 Intergalactic Social Media Bonanza 35
8 Human Trafficking 39
9 Misconstrued Messages of Candy and Tart Hearts 44
10 Fertummelt 46
11 We're Onions, Baby! 49
12 Chewy Didn't Roll Solo 51
13 Emotional Bingo 54
14 Windshield & Rear View 62
15 The Sixteen Year Old You 73
16 What's Your Dash? 75
17 Linear Equations 87
18 Recycle the Superficial 96
19 Ideas and Suggestions For Going Beyond 'The You' 99
20 Ingredients For Growth & Some Basic Rules For Life 101
21 Self Harm 103
22 Just Say No 106
23 The Socially Accepted Drug 120
24 Trends, Cycles and Patterns 124
25 Thus Saith the Drug Lady 128

About the Author

Erin Lawler Patterson provides weekly insights into the world of raising teens, mental health and family dynamics through her blog, Goodness Chick.

She is also a motivational speaker to parents, students and government officials willing to provide coffee and a bagel.

Check the goodness out:

www.goodnesschick.com

Acknowledgements

This book is dedicated to the women in my life who have been nothing short of epic. You have encouraged, inspired and rocked my world. Thank you for that.

To Mom....
For giving me life, never sugar coating anything and being my favorite morning phone call for the past fourteen years.

My sisters....
Jess, for inspiring me through your heart that is selfless, pure and beautiful. I love you for-e-ver.

Shana, my heart will ache with your absence until we are reunited in Heaven. You taught me to laugh, take risks and wring the crap out of every ounce of life.

To my kindred spirit, Carrie...
You are the walking definition of friendship. We've laughed until we've peed and we've cried until our sleeves were damp from snot. You are my Goose, baby!

To Mama Blong....
You're my sounding board, encourager and second mom. Thanks for being rad.

Thoughts from the Drug Lady

For the past thirteen years, I have held the title of Substance Awareness Coordinator at a high school in Southern New Jersey. My focus is on addiction, but in a day nothing is off limits. I work with the heavy hearted to those struggling with self-harm, eating, drug addiction, divorce, anger, sexual identity, anxiety and bullying; the list goes on. Thirteen years ago I was offered a job, congratulated, hugged and welcomed with open arms to a world that I had pretty minimal experience in. My first year I was constantly overwhelmed and freaked out at what I didn't know and what books simply had not prepared me for. I smiled and unknowingly agreed to start one of the most unpredictable, exciting, frightening and faith provoking chapters in my life.

I am the drug lady. Every morning I enter an emotional battlefield. It is with my heart that I strive to hear and with my eyes to reach out to the broken and unheard. There are moments in my day where hurt and sadness can feel all consuming. It is intense and crazy, but I consider myself blessed to have the privilege to work with the hearts of teenagers. I have the best job in the world.

The truth is that there are thousands upon thousands of mental health professionals out there fighting the same battle every day hoping, striving to make a difference and comfort the broken and down trodden. I guess you could say we're the emotional doctors suturing the mental fractures, brokenness and shattered hearts and spirits.

In today's world there are so many hurting and aching that it can be a daunting task. There are days you're on a natural high from an awesome session or successful intervention and there are others where you feel like you've had the wind knocked out of you, but man it's nothing short of a gift working with kids.

It's an amazing journey working with teenagers. There are moments that my mind wanders off to what it would be like to bake cookies or crunch numbers where emotional unpredictability isn't in the air. Working with kids is awesome. I have learned more from my interaction, counseling and mentoring teenagers than from any lecture or self-help book. Every day has become another lesson to apply to some facet of life. It's pretty fascinating when we are able to use our every day experiences as a tool for growth and learning.

So many of our kids are hurting; life happens. There are some who get a much worse hand in life than others, but our issues are our own no matter how big or small. The grass may or may not seem greener on the other side, but the plot of grass is your own and whatever the individual chooses to do with it is very often, but not always, up to them. If these issues are left alone to fester, they only manifest themselves into problems when the tweaks, bruises and bumps in the road aren't addressed. It seems only natural to keep plugging away, pretending or possibly going forward as a means of self-preservation. The problem only becomes more acute if there is no allocated time for trying to sort the fractured pieces out; it leads to a personal foundation that is fragmented making it all the more difficult for establishing a solid future. This doesn't mean every little bump and challenge needs to be explored, but it is imperative to address issues throughout different stages in life. When we delay and avoid dealing with our "stuff" it festers, simmers and snowballs then manifesting itself in negative ways.

The truth is that many of the lessons and themes of youth cross over into the genre of adulthood. Some of us are able to face our baggage and struggles head on while others are not. We have a funny way of rationalizing what we do and don't need to deal with. We make excuses. No one particularly likes to jump into their personal gook and sort through the good, the bad and the in between. The cool thing is, when we take that first step in defining who we are and figuring out what does and doesn't matter we actually begin to think a little clearer and the mind has a less overstuffed feel to it. I'll start off saying that I am not the most refined of individuals. I'm more up on surf conditions than stocks. I'm more comfortable in my Reef flip-flops than high heels. There are surfboards and camping chairs in my office with crisis hotline numbers taped to my filing cabinet. There is no prospect of either Harvard or Princeton contending for my employment anytime soon, but I'm content with that.

I grew up in a small town in southern New Jersey that was nestled away and wasn't really on the grid. It was a nice place to grow up. The high school I attended was in a fairly affluent area and as fate would have it, I currently live less than five miles away from where my childhood home once stood. My parents moved from north Jersey with hopes of a slower pace and what they believed would offer a better quality of life for my sisters and I.

From freshman to senior year of high school my perception of life and priorities shifted significantly. I lived in a great school district, but I found myself growing frustrated and annoyed with how cutthroat academics and athletics were. It wasn't that I didn't like high school, but the more I was exposed to soup kitchen visits in the city, visiting the elderly in retirement homes and other outreach projects, all the superficial crap turned my stomach. Getting my hands and heart involved in things that mattered was life altering. If I had taken the time to examine the faces and hearts I interacted with on a daily basis I would have realized that there was great need and hurt among my peers and throughout my community. No matter how glittery and bedazzled a community is there has been and always will be hurt just like every other small town across the nation; some needs are more discreetly hidden than others.

Bottom line: what you see is what you get with me. So, with that I proceed to write this book from my heart more than referring to therapeutic or pharmaceutical terminology. This comes from my perspective and personal experience with no intention of proclaiming fact or statements backed by research studies. I share my life experiences, views and perceptions with hope that it impacts a few hearts. As my Uncle Meyer used to say, "*It is what it is.*" In all my time in school I have gained the most knowledge walking the halls of an average American high school and my many ventures thousands of miles from home backpacking and living in places many couldn't find on a map. Some of life's most profound lessons are found in how we live our lives and how and when we choose to listen. These are my life lessons that I pass on to you, the reader.

Being Presently Present

Many of us face daily challenges waging battles against anxiety, depression, sadness, addiction, the shackles of their past, unhealthy relationships, etc. There's a whole lot of heartbreak out there. The truth is that most of us have struggles and challenges we would love to see change, but very few are willing to take the steps in transitioning from wanting something to change to actually taking the initiative in making change become a reality. There is verbal acknowledgement with the issue at hand, often conveyed numerous times over the course of weeks or months, but there's a firm resistance in going any further. The discontentment and host of emotions may even be clearly conveyed, but come to a grinding halt when action is required.

I want to change. I don't like how I react in particular situations. I would like to have healthy relationships. I'm not happy and haven't been in a long time. Having expectations or desires to tweak certain areas of our lives isn't abnormal. We should always be striving for growth and health in all facets of our lives, but too often we flap our lips or spin our mental wheels without ever doing anything about it. Sometimes talking is more of an action than for the individual and nothing ever goes beyond this. AAAAHHHHHH!!! Life's too short to flap...do something.

Whether it's in the capacity of either friend or clinician, I see the hamster in the wheel effect almost on a daily basis. There is a whole lot of running, exerting and chasing without any progress. Hearts are in a stand still with emotions and circumstances creating a sense of uncertainty making stopping or hopping off the wheel seem overwhelmingly frightening.

As humans, our present state cripples us. Peering outside of the scope is petrifying. But, it is possible. There comes a point where we cannot be forced, but rather we must choose to take the hand that is extended out to us, make that phone call, fall on our knees or seek out that which is beyond what we can do for ourselves. Whether it's depression, cutting, an addiction, anxiety perpetual fears, eating disorders or a million other things, there are options for help.

In a day and age with so many luxuries that were created to make our lives easier, sometimes there is the expectation that something or someone else will come along to do the dirty work for us in making change happen. Laziness and apathy reinforce the hamster wheel status. It's easy to talk about what needs to happen and how we will see ourselves in the future (either emotionally, financially, socially, etc.), but it's a whole different ball game to initiate. Life, change and taking that first step can be super frightening. What is even more alarming is when the talk is greatly outweighed by action and words are mere fluffy puffs of steam emitted from the lips. The illusion of what we will be must not be outweighed by the ability to move towards what we can be.

I worked with a young man who struggled with anger and it was starting to have direct consequences on his life impacting his academics and relationships with his family and friends. Peers and family members were also beginning to respond to him differently because of his shift in behavior and attitude. He was an awesome kid who just had a whole lot of 'spring cleaning' to do. Years of prolonged dealing with different forms of loss, stress and frustration in life allowed for an unhealthy form of anger to swell and eventually seep into all areas of his life. He was unhappy and wanted to change.

So often I've had kids in my office semi-listening and semi-desiring to change. This guy listened, paused and said, "*Lawler, how do I change? I'm not happy and I want to fix it.*" Bam! I made a list with just a few, simple doable things that were more of my test to see if this kid was more than just talk. Exactly one week later, the time frame I had given him, he stopped by my office first thing in the morning. From that point on I knew this guy meant business. Every time I saw him the wheels were spinning and he was hungry to get healthy, real and stoked for life. By the year's end I couldn't have been any prouder of the guy. He had goals, desires and 'to-dos' that allowed him to take a step back and challenge himself to grow and disallow any form of settling or excuse making.

Change isn't easy and very often it can't be checked off a list, but growth and willingness to just take that very first step is critical in our lives not becoming stagnant and hamster in a wheel like. Get off the wheel. Stop the wheel. Help, self-care, counseling or re-aligning requires personal initiative, but nothing happens overnight. Most of us aren't patient and in a day and age of instant access to everything we also have a tendency to have a personal time frame of how long we give 'help' to work before we become frustrated. A lot of times, it can be a lifelong process. That's not a bad thing, but rather a life focused on healing and realigning.

It can be hard sometimes to look ourselves in the mirror and like what we see. Life can be tough, rough and sometimes feel like we're its personal punching bag. But help, encouragement and long-term resources are out there. It's just taking that first, very scary, but very possible first step. Don't allow fear to keep you fixed in a rut of life. You're worth more than that and life is too fleeting to maintain rut status.

Words from a few graduates:

Change requires taking some form of initiative!

"Counseling was readily available in my high school, but the counselor doesn't take the first step. It's the student's decision to walk into the office."

"Before high school I thought that counseling was for people who couldn't get their lives together on their own. After meeting my high school counselor, I realized how natural and normal counseling is. It doesn't have to be awkward or superficial. It can be real and down to earth."

"School counseling was a nice baby step into seeing my current psychologist who I continue to see today. Counseling has helped me more than I could have ever imagined and it's something I recommend to anyone. You will learn more about yourself than you'll ever know."

We have to be the ones to initiate change and want it more than whoever may be encouraging us to make an effort to change. It can be done, but you have to take the first step.

Laundry Cycles

Part of the inability to step forward in connecting thought with action has to do with our clouded state of thinking. Focus and clarity of mind are definitely not overrated. We can drive ourselves nothing short of crazy wondering why our thoughts are in a million directions. We're tough on ourselves and often critical of why our minds seem incapable of staying in one place. It becomes the mental version of catching fire flies; you see one and clamor, but in the meantime a dozen more little flickering lights catch your attention in a dozen other directions.

Why is focus and balance such a challenge for so many of us? The answer: our load of laundry is overflowing. If you're not guilty of my next analogy, I commend you. For the rest of us, a raise of hands to the laundry over stuffers. You know who you are. The dial is cranked to super wash and in go the socks, underwear, tee shirts, jeans, pajamas and whatever else can make it in with the lid closing properly. We stuff it in, maybe even add a little more detergent to convince ourselves that we're actually doing one load of wash.

When the spinning and washing have come to an end we open the lid and wonder how in the world our thirty-two pieces of wash have now morphed into one solid, totally tangled object? The undoing of socks and shirts, sweats and pajamas is a frustrating process. But what did we really think was under that lid after the final spin? Some of us open the lid with a wince; others open it up seemingly shocked at the unfortunate nature of their findings. *Dude, you put two point three washes into one. What did you think was going to happen?* The funny thing is the super wash wasn't even truly washed effectively. What? That extra detergent couldn't really do what it was intended to because of the lack of space to circulate and that there was just simply not enough water, space and detergent to do what it was intended to. Bummer.

Our minds are really pretty similar to that super wash. We go in stuffing in a little of the following: *what are we making for dinner, making sure we remind ourselves when the utility bill is due, is paperwork up to date with the last client, did that text to Jen come across the wrong way, why am I having headaches all the time, did Dad get his tests done for those chest pains he was having and I need to make a note for myself to call about Greg's dentist appointment?* It's a little bit of a whole lot of things. Obligations, goals, responsibilities and concerns of past and present are all parts of our lives and things we cannot permanently extract from our life's load of laundry. The problem is when it is all circulating, spinning and stuffed in at the same time.

We wonder why we have headaches, chest pains or the inability to tack down one fluid thought process? Again and again our cycle is on super wash. It isn't fair and frustration builds, but we are relentless in just giving it a go one more time thinking, maybe I can get away with it this time? But we can't. Quality of life is affected. Vulnerability to being emotionally on edge heightens. Lethargy and a sense of 'numbness' can seep in. We are tiring ourselves out with the simple concept of thinking, thinking, thinking.

How can we set it all to a different wash cycle? Is it even possible? Yes. But it goes against our natural wiring where it takes time, patience and consistency. These are three things that aren't part of most of our genetic make-up. It starts with organizing our thoughts. It's taking the time to jot down 'to dos' that are accessible yet not just swarming around in our heads. It's allocating a little bit of time daily to be still and giving our brains a reprieve.

Being still and breathing exercises are a start in attempting to clear out some of the clutter making an effort at barricading even more stuff from seeping in. It's the little steps that go far: waking up twenty minutes earlier for a time of prayer, stillness void of cell phone or television, having a cup of coffee in silence before the world stirs, driving with the radio off, windows cracked a bit with three and a half minutes of giving thanks and being absent of crazy even if for two hundred and ten seconds. It can be allowing yourself to actually enjoy the now; not thinking about yesterday or tomorrow, just being in the moment. That might mean putting down the cell phones, making eye contact and talking about the day. It could be as simple as sitting in your backyard, on your porch or in the park and watching the stars or leaves change. Maybe letting the wind hit your hair when you're driving or enjoying the feel of a light rain on your face.

You may think these all seem crazy, unattainable or insignificant. The truth of it is, so many of us have allowed the beauty of the now to slip through our hands. We are so crazy with past, present and future it all becomes one clump of laundry that seems impossible to untangle. Life is crazy. There are seasons in life that can be heartbreaking, painstaking and life shattering. There are also other seasons that bring life, beauty and joy. It is up to us as to whether we take opportunities to sort our laundry and choose what goes in and what doesn't.

I've had many times in my life where the super wash is on and the clothes are stuffed to capacity. I feel it. It impacts all facets of my life. The de-stuffing process isn't an easy one. It can be a life long struggle. The truth is when we begin to make it a priority and we become more aware of what is and isn't deemed necessary to overwhelm us with, the wash load becomes lighter and change takes place over time. Life's too short to be on super wash all the time.

A heartbreaking aspect is how so many of our kids are being set to an overload wash cycle from the time they can walk. We are now beginning to see the outcome of a generation of kids with cleats strapped on at the age of five for soccer while quickly removing their jersey in exchange for an apron for art class, inhaling dinner at the table or in the car just in time to return home to half consciously complete homework before passing out to do it over again the next day. Being involved and active is important, but the problem is too often our kids are being stretched too thin and they experience a level of stress and angst that is just simply unnecessary.

There are populations of five to eighteen year olds that are not being allowed to be kids. Maybe it's the drive of having what we didn't as kids. It could be the desire to have them be as well rounded as humanly possible. Honestly, it could be a million things. At five or eleven, schlepping from point A to point B to point D back to point A isn't healthy. Being a part of activities/ sports/clubs is fun and important, but it's making that careful judgment call of where the balance is and isn't being maintained and, sometimes, that's not always an easy decision. I live in a neighborhood where kids ride their bikes to school, neighbors take their after dinner walks around the lake and date night can be found at the local ice cream shop a quarter mile up the road. But even in my little niche of a world that seems light years away, there is a noticeable decline in the outside, in the street, "Kids being kids" kind of world.

There was a time that you would get home from school, throw your book bag down, go outside to play and you weren't allowed back in until it was time for dinner. There was a street hockey, tree climbing, fort building, pick-up soccer playing kind of world. I know it still exists in different pockets of our communities, but there is a limited amount of time where our kids can breathe deeply, get dirty and be kids. Part of that has changed with safety concerns and a whole myriad of other issues, but our kids are being wired too tightly with a skewed perception of what it is to be a kid. Throw in the laptop, Facebook, Snap Chat, iPhone, Twitter and Instagram and you have a few more tidbits distracting and detracting from kids very simply being kids.

Every fall I hop on a bus with approximately twenty-five to thirty teenagers and four or five teachers for a three day retreat in Virginia. It's a six-hour trip that forces all of us away from all and any obligations to the outside world. I feel profoundly blessed to have the opportunity to work with these kids for three point days absent from the outside world's distractions. These guys are all upper classmen in high school who have gone through a five -week training with me about life, character and decision-making. The retreat is a follow-up to training. Most of these kids are very involved with clubs, activities, work, life, etc. They're great kids, just very typical over stretched young people. I have to admit, this is one of the highlights of my year. The kids are stoked about what's ahead, but can't really get it until they get it.

From the time we leave there are ice-breakers, challenges and group activities where they are totally removed from their environment. I do not allow cell phone use unless it is necessary to contact home. I encourage them to step away from social media, texting with friends, and so on for this sixty hour window of their lives. Initially, the crew isn't ecstatic about their cell phone disconnect from the world.

What's really neat is to see when there is less social networking distractions combined with an inability to do anything outside of what's going on in the moment there are so many positives that transpire. These kids are forced to interact, chat, take a walk down to the lake, have hot chocolate by the fire engaged with someone they really never had taken the time to know or hop on a swing and feel the wind through their hair. They are forced to be still, relax and breathe. I love it. You can actually see the stress and distraction melt away as peace and joy sets in. The barriers initially present sort of fizzle and these young people are able to jump into a depth of discussion and personal challenge because time permitted it. They begin taking the time to think about who they are, how they are living as well as dealing with different aspects of life they may have not looked at before.

The laundry begins to get sorted and the weight in their eyes becomes lighter. I believe, with all of my heart, that we need time for us. Taking time to just be. Allowing for real relationships and stillness is something necessary at different parts of our life. When we get mired in things that cloud our thoughts and passions it takes a toll.

I have witnessed young people's lives change over this very short period of time. There are some who dismiss what is said, that's to be expected. Others who challenge themselves reconsidering if their laundry loads are too full an, if so, what needs to be altered. When we listen and re-evaluate some pretty cool things can happen. Three and a half days in the middle of nowhere might not be feasible, but an hour here and there is and must be. Finding creative ways to regroup and recharge is not only healthy, but it can be fun seeking out new ways to get a little down time.

We have to take a step back and allow the wash to be less packed. There is something special about having designated meal time with the ones you love learning to sit still, appreciate and communicate. Instilling the fact that sports aren't everything. The likely hood of transitioning from middle school super star to NBA legend is near impossible and grades are pretty important, but it's character and communication that creates the person.

We just simply have to switch gears a bit and be less inclined to juggle more than we can handle. If we have kids starting out over juggling and over stressing at such an early age we are bound to have a future generation of angst ridden adults who will struggle to be the healthy balanced people they are meant to be.

<-----A FEW WAYS TO CHILL IN 24 HOURS------>

Sing your favorite song while in the shower. Have a hot cup of tea or coffee. Roll your neck in a circle switch directions while closing your eyes for thirty seconds. Soak your feet in a salt bath for ten minutes. Call an old friend and let yourself laugh and reflect. Burn a candle that reminds you of chill and goodness. Take your socks off and walk on sand or grass. Drive with your windows down or cracked and take in some fresh air. Sit and watch the stars. Hold hands with someone you love. Swing on a swing. Lay on carpet and stretch your arms and feet and breathe deep a half dozen times. Hug someone you appreciate. Watch an old show that reminds you of being a kid. List ten things that you are grateful for.

Words from a graduate:

"I've started to appreciate my personal mental health more. Being in college is a totally different environment and it can really stress your health both physically and mentally. I've learned how to take more time for me and to appreciate myself. I've definitely matured with regards to this and learned to take some of the pressure off of myself."

Don't be a Stubby Candle

Is it our wiring? Could it be our inability to sit still? Is it a fear of equating down time with laziness? A core element of scattered stress brain is from our society and culture. Go, go, go and stuff that wash and have it dried, folded and put away in a limited time with even more limited resources. We're burning the candle at both ends. Stubby candles can't emit light and have no real practical use. *Just say no to stubby candle status.*

It was in Monticello Amiata, nestled in the valley of Tuscany, that I realized that my drive to succeed and accomplish was removing the ability to enjoy the simplicities of life. There were too many to do lists in my head detracting from the pleasures around me.

A week after graduating from college I hopped on a plane and headed to Europe. I literally walked from my graduation ceremony to a bank where I took out a five thousand dollar loan to sort of find myself. I remember the banker asking me what I had as collateral. My ten year- old jeep and three surfboards didn't make the cut, go figure. As cliché as it sounds, it was a journey I needed desperately. I was working part time for North Carolina's Governor's office on Drug & Alcohol Research. I had multiple opportunities for employment at my fingertips. There was a great, secure road ahead and everyone I knew thought I was crazy for shedding the securities of my life in exchange for an endless road of 'what ifs.' It was one of the most liberating chapters in my life that changed me in more ways than I could have ever imagined.

A good amount of my time abroad was spent in Italy working on farms as a WWOOFer (Willing Workers on Organic Farms), essentially a farm hand. I went from a gig in Southern Ireland working as a transcriber at the University of College Cork to a farm in Monticello Amiata in the heart of Tuscany. I was twenty-two, full of energy and low on common sense. But life is about learning after all, isn't it? Marta, owner of the first farm I worked on, was a short, wiry Italian woman with leather brown skin, weather blown chestnut brown hair and a fiend for non-filtered cigarettes.

WWOOF is about providing a cultural experience for all involved, but Marta had a different agenda. She intended to dole out as little as possible and in return work those visiting to the core. When I first arrived I was introduced to Grant and Gina, an American couple from California. We hit it off instantly as did I with the three others who happened to be local Italians assisting with a handful of projects on the farm. Maximillian, Guiseppi and Paolo were what you would consider your old-school Italians possessing a charm and love for life that was contagious. The first night of my stint on Marta's compound was spent getting acquainted with all the workers over a few carafes of red wine, good cigars and a solid game of poker.

It had been a long day reaching my destination. My trek to Marta's was an entire day of hopping on and off buses, holding incomprehensible conversations (my Italian vocabulary consisted of approximately fifteen words which was pretty comparable to Marta's fifteen words of English) on a public pay phone (remember those?) with my future farm furor. Every hour that passed without connecting to my destination I prayed a little harder while struggling to hold back tears. I had no idea where I was and although the map in my back pocket had her town circled in dark black ink, it meant nothing at a payphone in a town that wasn't on my map. Marta didn't recruit young workers with the intention of providing a cultural experience, but more of getting free labor with minimal output on her part. Once I actually reached my destination the day of trekking on foot, schlepping on numerous buses and attempting to be coherent in Italian had taken it's toll and I was unconscious before my body even hit the bed.

The next morning there was a chill in the air as I opened the green shutters from my bedroom door letting the sun's rays spill onto the cold tile floor. It was like something out of a movie: trickling brook, chirping birds and rolling hills with a blanket of lush green grass. It was fantastic. I had flipped through books and albums that focused on Tuscany, but none of them did this place justice. It was surreal. But the magic was short lived.

Within the first three minutes of sitting in the pick-up truck with Marta the prior night I had a gut feeling that she was not adding me to her top ten list of favorite people. She worked Grant, Gina and I more intensely as the days went on. Tasks ranged from clearing truckloads of brush off of sloping mountainsides to lugging huge rocks around the property to herding horses that seemed more familiar with charging than prancing. It was hard work. One morning I was instructed that I would be paired off with someone else. As I sipped my cappuccino and gnawed on a round of bread dipped in honey she informed me that I would be working with Ilario. I would have been absolutely content with that, no questions asked, if it weren't for Gina and Grant's facial reaction. Eyebrows raised and awkward silence was a giveaway for trepidation to be had upon my meeting with Ilario.

I was told to head up to the highest point of the drive where Ilario would already be working. Walking along the gravel drive I attempted to push out words such as old and grumpy that had been used to describe my new work partner. From twenty yards away I could hear the distinct sound of a shovel piercing the hard earth followed by a subtle grunt. He couldn't have been more than five foot three with a mat of white hair contained by a worn gray painter's cap. His jeans were tattered and his gray sweater clung to his solid frame. I knew he was aware that I was approaching, but he didn't acknowledge me for an eternal stretch of a minute or so. When I stood beside him, he made final touches with his shovel around a Cyprus tree and wiped his brow and straightened his back.

His eyes were a deep crystal blue and his face was tanned. The wrinkles on his face seemed telling of the life he had lived, what he had seen and endured. He caught me off guard extending his hand with a very stern, "*Bongiorno.*" The words to follow were rapid, incomprehensible. Ilario spoke not a lick of English and I knew no more than a few dozen or so words and phrases in Italian. He furrowed his brown as he realized what I had already known, we couldn't communicate and yet we had the next week or so to plant a countless number of Cyprus trees along the perimeter of the property. Without hesitation he walked over to his opey (three wheeled pick-up) and returned with a shovel.

Communication is much more than words. Through body language, facial expressions and even the subtle sigh so much is conveyed. I knew we had a lot ahead of us and as I began shoveling one scoop after another of dirt I realized there was only one shovel moving. Here it was that Ilario was leaning against his shovel observing me. I shrugged my shoulders and he walked over, removed the shovel that I was grasping with both hands and waved for me to follow him. I went as instructed. He leaned both shovels against his truck and reached into the bed of the opey and removed an old rusted tool box. Ilario sat on the bed of the truck and patted for me to sit next to him as he propped open the tool box taking out an unlabeled bottle of red wine, cheese covered with a small towel, a round of bread and a half a stick of pepperoni. This guy and I were going to get along just fine.

On the tailgate of that opey I learned some of life's greatest lessons that will stay with me as long as I live. As we chatted I kept looking at my watch as I had this strange misperception that time was getting the best of us. Ilario placed his hands in mine, removed my watch delicately with his calloused fingers and placed it in the toolbox. As he grinned he said, *"no good."* A little English goes a long way. We sat in silence for the next hour and although I had been on the farm for some time it was the first time I recognized the profound beauty of this place. The stone home with a stucco roof in the middle of a valley of rolling hills, picturesque lines of olive trees and blades of wheat that seemed to sway with the shifting of the wind. The sun, golden and seeming to stretch its rays along the horizon, warmed my face. *I think too much. My mind races too often and there is a propensity to look ahead of me instead of the now. Why is that? What's the rush? There will be tomorrow, but there will never be another today.* As I sat there it was the first time in my life that I had hit the breaks on my brain and the pause button on life and was just there and living in the moment.

Ilario and I returned to work and every now and then he would touch my arm and say,*"Lentamente. Lentamente, Erin"* (he and all Italians pronounced my name as E-ll-in). He may have had an intimidating exterior, but in a few short hours his shell was shed and Ilario had really taken me under his wing and exposed a softer side I would never had guessed existed. As he chided words that I couldn't tell you what they meant I still knew exactly what he was saying through his tone and persistence. You don't always need words to get the point across and the heart's intent can breach farther than what is spoken. Just as I had preconceived notions about him before even exchanging words, I'm sure he did for me as well. What I now attempt to be more conscious of is how I present myself and how open I am regardless of language, skin color, culture, dress or economic status. So much of the outside is just a façade; it really doesn't matter.

Lentamente. Lentamente. I knew it would leave his lips before it was spoken as dusk settled in. I now wanted it to go beyond words and begin to sink in. Was I willing to be challenged to look at myself by the prompting of an old Italian farmer? You betcha. How many of us need the occasional reminder to take a brief step back from the intensity of life and take a few breaths? There will always be responsibility, an item on the to do list of our post-it pile and another phone call to return. But there will not always be today and even the ones we love the most aren't guaranteed forever. We sort of have a tendency to take so much of the richness around us for granted. It all becomes sand slipping through our fingertips; hold onto it for even a few moments before it's gone.

At the end of my first day with Ilario I returned to the house. After a hot shower, I headed out to the patio to have a glass of wine with Grant and Gina who I knew would be curious of day's events. But my mind was full of a richness and appreciation in away it had never been before and it seemed impossible to attach words to it. As we watched the sun setting over the Tuscan landscape, I sat in silence listening to their day. *"Ok Er, fill us in; how did it go?"* I smiled, *"Awesome."* I stood up and very casually said, *Oh, and we have a dinner invite at Ilarios. I'm going to get dressed. We have to be there by seven."* The combination of silence and the blank stares on their faces made it difficult to hold back from laughing out loud. It was priceless. So dinner it was and as the three of us trekked the one- mile uphill climb towards town; I was seeing Tuscany in a whole new light. Darkness covering the valley below with the flickering of candles and lights from the house below and homes above perched along the hilltop. There was such stillness and beauty and warmth that resonated from the homes along the great and mighty hilltop.

That evening I broke bread with Grant, Gina, Ilario, his brother Guiseppi and about a half dozen of their best friends from grade school. As we sat around a picnic table in their garage, I couldn't understand any of the conversation, but I didn't need to. The men around me were in their late sixties. There was the butcher, the baker, the grocer and Ilario and his brother, the wine and olive oil connoisseurs. None of these men had ever left Italy and I might even venture to say the region of Tuscany. No one would recognize them outside of their town, but here, this was their world where there was a history, depth and a level of purity in their relationships that I had never witnessed before. They did not have cell phones connected to their hips. They didn't hang out at internet cafes or dash out to their next appointment with a Starbucks in their hand. It was like life freeze -framed and I didn't find it strange, but wildly alluring.

On our walk home the three of us were not in search of words, but instead sat on the hedge of a stonewall overlooking our home below in silence. It's easy to talk, but much harder to listen and even harder yet to take the time to sort out the swirling mess that can be found in the human mind. I didn't even know Ilario twenty- four hours ago and there I was facing some of the greatest struggles of my life due to his prompting.

We're all layered and complex which is OK, but if we lose sense of who we are, it's near impossible to be healthy and productive in mind and body. It's keeping tabs that the layers don't become walls disallowing healthy relationships along with taking time to take care of ourselves. But it is time that is a whole other issue.

It's funny how life works. I had to travel across the Atlantic before I grasped that: a) I don't know everything b) I never will c) life can't always be Tuscany, but it can have its Tuscan like moments d) life's greatest treasures are closer than you think. As I sat under the watchful eye of Ilario there was so much I learned about myself. *Why do I rush, why do I live for tomorrow and have this very compartmentalized view of life?*

It has been more than fifteen years since I've last seen or spoken to Ilario, but I can picture the old man and his opey like it were yesterday. There have been moments in my life where I've transported myself back to a place that seemed utopian. Every once in a while there will be a gentle, sweet breeze that fills the air and as I close my eyes I'm transported back to that field of swaying wheat, buzzing bees, the babbling creek and the old man waving in the distance. It all seems a lifetime ago, but I was there and the images, colors and faces will stay embedded in my heart until I leave this earth. At the time I didn't realize the true richness of what I had, but how could I really?

Tuscany is now something that I carry with me forever. It's in my heart and there are times that a priority check is needed and the chiding of Ilario's gentle voice echoes in my mind. Taking time, being centered and allowing a little lentamente go a long way because it really can if we allow it to.

If we make ourselves, even in the smallest of ways, more of a priority it's amazing how the wick isn't burning at both ends with the nubby, stubby candle becoming ever more irrelevant. It isn't about prioritizing in a self-serving way, but with the intention of clearing out the muddled laundry to allow for a purer form of life that in so many ways allows for a healthier way of conducting our lives at home, work and on a social level. From making lists, enjoying the little moments in our day that can so easily slip through our fingertips to allocating a few moments to breathe and be still. These are all efforts to function and think in a way that will inevitably allow for a higher quality of life.

Blades of wheat move in
   motion
with a breeze
   that is not contained
    by a minute hand
     or what hour of the day it is
      Beauty, reprieve found
       when pause is had
      and eyes are opened
     to a beauty, a rest that so
   easily and so often
is simply overlooked

Haitian Perspective

When it comes to our cluttered minds, there is a connection to an issue that's deeper than soccer practices and lattes. There is a cultural wave of discontentment. This breaks down to who we are, our personal inventory of what we do or do not possess, along with the labels we may or may not have that we can equate to self-worth. Hearts caught up in keeping up with the Jones's or the simple reality of having so much in the material context and yet being so emotionally unsatisfied. It's a truth about American culture that is hard to dispute. In comparison to other countless countries around the globe we are dripping with excess, yet so many are so unhappy with what is in their possession.

There are many pockets of the United States where people live paycheck to pay check, who are forced to live in their cars instead of a home and their only means of meeting three square meals a day is relying on their local food banks. Starbucks and Apple laptops aren't part of their world and running water and heat are more of a concern. This is not the population that I focus on, instead it is those with a broader fixation of wanting, desiring for more and ongoing accumulation.

There are countries in the midst of coups, financial chaos and lacking the opportunity that so many are allotted in the United States of America and other first world countries. The vast majority of those in the Western World live in conditions far beyond what those in all walks of the globe could even imagine. While we may gripe about slow wifi service, our barista not making a quality macchiato or the grumbles we spew with those missing pair of sunglasses; we have neighbors walking the same soil without running water, wi-fi access or an area TJ Maxx or Anthropology for the newest styles of clothing. It's foreign in so many ways. I am not bashing possessions, but rather the hunger instilled of not being satisfied. The lack of contentment that surrounds so much of our culture is evident everywhere you turn.

It's not wrong to desire more for yourself, but there is a line where want supersedes need and the balance is lost.

A few years ago while spending the day in an orphanage outside of Port O Prince, Haiti there were a group of children playing soccer in a field with patches of grass, no nets in sight and a heat index of "I am hallucinating and perpetually parched." These kids were orphans, living in a fourth world country, attending school under tattered tarps with faded UNICEF symbols on each side while laying their heads down at night on what I can only very loosely describe as beds. Yet, in the two weeks we played on the playground, kicked soccer balls and did a ton of arts and crafts not once did one child we encountered complain. Not once did an adult do anything other than sit and dialogue about our lives back home and what they were doing there in Haiti. There were smiles and an authentic contentment with where they were (not saying they did not have goals and aspirations) that I found so fascinating.

It took every ounce of self -control to not cry and fall to my knees with a heavy heart walking around their living quarters. Children living at the orphanage had neither a mom nor a dad or those whose parents had no choice but to give their child up in hopes of a better future with a roof over their heads and food in their tummies. Kids who sat in oppressive heat under a makeshift schoolhouse playing in what we would consider a mound of dust in a country plagued by poverty and political corruption. There were no Chick Fil-A's. There were no desserts after dinner or big screen TV to play XBOX before heading to bed, but every single kid hugged, thanked and smiled at the volunteers who were mere visitors for a fleeting moment in their lives. What their futures held was unknown. Unemployment and poverty was and still is the norm, but there is an effort to educate the younger population to break this cycle. Even in the midst of this uphill battle, there is a hope and peace that is not founded in materials.

"Miss Erin, play with me!"
A little boy, no more than six or seven,
tugged at my shirt with one hand
while pointing at the swings with the other
His skin, as black as night,
seemed to glow against the Haitian sun
And his eyes sparkled with a joy
that made my heart skip a beat
With a smile of pink chapped lips
and a few missing teeth
that left little thought but to follow him
along the arid path leading to the creaky swings
The pint sized wonder must have stretched
as arms and legs reached for the clouds
Faster, higher he yelled
in between laughs and catching his breath
Everything about this moment was perfect
and uninhibited by the fact
That he didn't have breakfast this morning
His laughter was uncontrollable
His young, perfect hands stretched
trying with all his might to catch clouds
There was no mention of having to walk a half-mile
to bring fresh water to the
over-hang he called home later in the day
No comment of not having any colored pencils
or markers to start school in a few weeks
Only pleads to keep swinging
Playing until the sunset
Every push of the swing my hands trembled
My one hand wanted to save him
from what the future held for him

The other hand wanted to bottle up his joy, love for life
and keep it close to my heart
Tattered shorts and an unblemished heart provided
lessons for a lifetime
Miss Erin, I jump now!
And without hesitation he let go
without time to heed warning
I watched my little professor jump so high
and so mightily
That just for a moment, he blocked the sun
and filled the sky with hands, feet and smile

I'm not sure if the key is less is more or if it's a heart issue. Learning to be still, find peace and a sense of contentment with what one has or does not have is a challenge. But I believe this unhealthy state contributes to generations of young and old who struggle with being still and at peace with wherever they may be. What stems from this can be sadness, anxiety and a host of other unsettled states. But once it's recognized, it can be something the heart and mind can tackle. There's only room for improvement after all.

My head once spun in a million directions and there was never stillness within my inner core. My saving grace was realizing that I needed peace and an 'OK-ness' with myself that could only been rooted in my faith and personal relationship with Jesus Christ. I was a frolicking boat in some pretty crazy white caps until I made the decision to stop chasing things I didn't need to chase and realized stillness is a pretty cool and life altering state to be in. My faith was what corked the hole in my boat that was bound for overturning. I can say pretty confidently, that without my faith and my corked boat I'm fairly sure I would not be here today. I am profoundly grateful to a God who loves me unconditionally and has provided a hope and fullness that no material item or person could fill.

I believe that there are many hearts that are not satisfied and yearn for more. That can be a compulsion with academics, status, shoes, size of your house or position on a sport's team. There's nothing wrong with desires to succeed, live comfortably and provide for those we love. But what is wrong is when we use things as a means of defining our identity. Stuff and labels can't buy happiness.

I recommend to anyone out there to take a bit of time out of your schedule and volunteer at a soup kitchen, grab a hammer or broom when there's a Habitat for Humanity project going on in your area, donate a bag of food to your local food pantry or make a box of goodies with your loved ones to send to a man or woman over seas. In the course of a day there are so many opportunities to give of ourselves. The most precious gifts don't require money. It's allowing our perception of the hearts we come across to be perceived differently. It's pretty awesome to know we all have the ability to impact and enhance the hearts of others with just a little bit of time, seeking and courage in taking that first step.

My stay in Haiti was spent with Hope Alive Clinics. Please feel free to check out their web site: www.hopealiveclinic.org to gain some insight into the needs of the Haitian people and what you can do to legit save someone's life with a click of a button. How sweet is that?

R-E-S-P-E-C-T

Whether in the work place or on the beach chatting about politics has a tendency to leave me ridden with agita and angst. Blah. Regardless, I consider myself super blessed to have the ability to not only openly express my political stance, but I have the privilege to vote. Every day I dress how I see fit, drive my car without fear of an uprising and attend my place of worship with little concern for being patronized or accosted. Simple privileges that are beautiful freedoms; each were provided by the sacrifice of men and women since before our country was even founded. Blood, loss and sacrifice in exchange for our present freedoms; what a powerful truth this is.

War is an ongoing presence across the globe. Every day we have men and women from all branches serving, protecting and sacrificing. But we are in a day and age that isn't Vietnam or World War II. With loss not directly glaring us in the face there's been a dilution (for many, but not all) of what our country is all about, the sacrifices that have and continue to be made. Freedom is not free.

In my opinion, this disconnect has made for a very ungrateful and self-entitled generation. When we don't grasp that freedom is not a right, but a privilege and is granted through sacrifice its acute relevance is lost. Whether wearing a hat during the National Anthem, rolling one's eyes having to recite the Pledge of Allegiance or being a distraction while heads bow in a moment of silence, it's a lack of respect.

Some cool ways to gain insight into the layers and history of our country is to chat with vets and hear their stories and experiences. It's mind blowing. Whether the marine who recently returned from a tour in Afghanistan or the Navy vet who was there to storm the beaches of Normandy; these people are living history and it'll not only give you goose bumps, but legit make you want to buy a cup of coffee for every military person you come across. Stories that are full of color, experience and depth that provide an insight into who we are as a nation and how we arrived.

There are also countless individuals who paid the ultimate sacrifice and gave their lives for our freedom. A day we kind of need to tweak a bit is Memorial Day. We're inundated with commercials for epic sales on washers and dryers or clothing. There's the gazillion bags of chips and Fritos that will line red and white checkered tables over the three day weekend with cases of soda and beer to fuel hydration needs from sea to shining sea. We've become accustomed to greetings of *Happy Memorial Day* and *Have an awesome weekend* instead of having a heavier, more pensive heart going into the days ahead. The day wasn't founded on stoke, but being somber and paying respect. That's just my two cents.

I'm not sure where we lost touch with its real meaning, but we need to bring it back to its roots. There are so many faces and hearts who are not with their loved ones on the extra day off of work to recline, chill and grill. Memorial Day is etched in our calendars as a day to commemorate and remember those who have fallen. It's intended to be solemn, reflective and powerful. So even taking the day to be with family and friends, before eating and enjoying take a moment of silence. Remember those who have fallen.

Reflecting and appreciating make us better as a whole and as individuals. So as we honk the horn at the guy taking too long to move after the light has turned green or when frustrated at the line in the supermarket or while waiting for our macchiato at the local bean shop, all of these beautiful pleasures in life we enjoy without really connecting how we arrived here. We have freedoms that many across the globe can hardly fathom.

A number of years ago I spent six weeks trekking through the Middle East. Most of my time was spent in Israel, but the last leg of my trip had me crossing into the Sinai before heading towards Cairo. At the border I had encountered a few other backpackers and we made our way to a small town where a Swiss couple owned a number of huts situated along the shoreline that catered to backpackers. There were about two-dozen huts scattered along the shoreline with arid mountains and desert as the backdrop. It was stunning.

As Americans, I don't think most of us even pause about what we wear as we head out to the grocery store, movie-theater or park. Our dress is a part of our identity. When I travel abroad I do my utmost to adhere to the dress and culture. Throughout my Middle East and Egyptian venture my typical dress was a long linen skirt with flip-flops, a long sleeved linen shirt that covered most of my hands and a lightweight scarf that went over my head. My fingertips, feet and portions of my hands were visible. In Israel and Jordan this was never an issue, so I didn't think anything of venturing into the small town that was a five-minute walk from where I was staying.

The closest town consisted of maybe three dozen homes spread out and one convenience store. Sheep and dogs darted across the street as the sun's glare made the one hundred degree thermostat reading feel more like one thousand degrees. I ducked into the convenience store that couldn't have consisted of more than four aisles with worn wood flooring and the crackling blare of a boom box radio. The store appeared empty until my eyes met an older man sitting in the back corner of the store smoking a hookah pipe; he eyed me up and down at least six times in a way that made my skin crawl. I bolted down the first aisle that allowed me to gain my composure. The dim aisle stacked with boxes of fluoride toothpaste and jarred olives felt like it was narrowing with each step. I leaned my hands against the shelf. From what felt like inches away I heard, *"Whore. Infadel. Whore...."* My body spun around and my legs carried me out as my heart and stomach followed behind.

All I could do was run. I don't think I ever ran so fast in my life and there was no way I was looking back. If I was taken, snatched up no one would have ever known where I was or what had happened. In this part of the world my dress, the showing of skin and eye contact equated to being dirty and loose. A scary level of insane that left my hands shaking, my heart in my throat and a fear I had never experienced before. I am thankful, grateful and so overly in awe of the freedoms we have in our great country. I was saturated in a freedom that I could not wrap my head around until that day where my dignity, safety and identity were instantly tossed to the wayside. Freedom to wear my jeans, tee shirt, sweatshirt and flip-flops is a freedom I am SO overly grateful for.

Every single day we wake up, dress, go about our day and live life in a way that is so easy to take for granted. Whether it be who we marry to chatting about politics around the water cooler or walking your kids to school in the morning, these are all freedoms, beautiful every day gifts that are easily taken for granted. Freedom, liberty and the gifts that we have as an American people have not and continue to not come without cost.

So during the next Memorial Day as you grill your burgers, work on your garden or talk politics over drinks, take a few minutes to pause and remember the meaning behind the day. There are thousands who won't have their mom, dad, best friend or cousin to play horse shoes with or sit around the fire pit at the end of a long day because their loved one paid the ultimate sacrifice. They gave their lives for our freedom. I am so very grateful to be an American, but particularly on Memorial Day. I am humbled to remember the countless who gave their lives for my freedoms. Freedom is not free. Take some time to remember and never forget.

Intergalactic Social Media Bonanza

Social media has made the world seem smaller allowing almost anything to be within a fingertip's touch away. With this instantaneous access, it has opened a floodgate of issues that are having direct implications on our young people. The constant need for the cell phone to always be on and present, the pull to check the latest posts on Twitter or Instagram has our kids (and many adults) demonstrating compulsive behaviors that are only on the rise with time.

In the past few years there has been a correlation between anxiety and social media. When eyes and minds are constantly fixed to and stimulated by tiny screens and vibrating texts it makes it challenging to detach. It is concerning when there is an uprising of young and old who struggle to function without their phones constantly with them. Being accustomed to constant instant access to texting, social media updates and the simple security found in having their phones with them at all times has become an issue. Without it literally attached to hand or hip there is a sense of loss and angst. With time and a new generation of young people saturated by social media and instant everything these issues will only increase. Fingers and minds can become almost all consumed with having instant access along with the underlying fear of being out of the social media loop even for a short span of time. If I identity and sense of worth is founded on likes, re-tweets and comments they are doomed for disappointment and heartache. Identity cannot be forged through social media.

It's easy to turn a blind eye to our kids being engrossed with their phones or computers, but there is tremendous danger in the unknown. Cyberspace has become an open doorway for a lot of scary stuff that our kids can enter unintentionally. The stark reality is that social media has opened the gateways for child predators to 'friend' through Facebook, Tinder or Twitter feeds under a false identity. There is the accessibility of hardcore pornography. When our kids are able to hide behind the screen of their phone or computer it sets the platform for issues such as posting the irretrievable photo from a party the night prior with a bong or scantily clothed young person or there's the innocent tweet on Twitter that quickly morphs into a ruthless bullying session. All of these are happening and the frequency is only increasing. This is compounded by the stark reality that our kids' brains are not fully developed. Here is where impulsivity can get them in over their heads without even realizing it, landing them in some very precarious situations.

I was a pretty good kid in high school, but I was a teenager and did plenty of dumb things. There were times I was impulsive, in the wrong place at the wrong time or just simply being stupid. I can confidently say that I would have posted at least one picture or status update of me in a place I should not have been, with peers doing things we should not have been engaging in. You couldn't pay me to be a teenager in today's world. There's too much out there. It's overwhelming. This is where parenting, guiding and educating our kids is critical. If we don't dialogue with them, then it is their peers who are providing their sole form of social media education and that scenario doesn't have a great outcome.

There are great kids out there, but regardless of good or bad, we are in a day and age where social media's presence is twenty-four seven. There are those who struggle with having constant access to their phones creating a noticeable rise in anxiety and compulsion attached to phones and social media. It's almost painful for some of our kids to go a fifty-five minute class period without the ability to 'check-in' via cell.

The worldwide web and the cell phone are not going away anytime soon. It's uncomfortable when we lament on what's out there; it is a scary world. What is more frightening is allowing our kids to navigate through uncharted waters. Over the years I've met with students who have had their hands over their face in tears saying, *"I wish I could take it back...,"* but with social media you can't. Lives and hearts have been impacted with the simple click of a button. It happens every day.

I believe there's power in knowledge and being pro-active. Talk with your young person. Are their Twitter, Facebook, Tinder, Instagram, and Finstagram (often used as a secondary more anonymous account) accounts set on open or private settings (meaning can the whole world have access to their information or is it limited to their friends)? Do whatever you can to be at least part of their social media world. Whether that's checking in on their networking sites, having access to their passwords (which I strongly encourage) or even being friends with them on whatever forms of social media they are on to have access to their information (even though they do have the ability to block you from particular posts). The truth is that the imminent possibility of Mom, Dad or guardian checking in on them deters impulsive behavior.

A few easy ways to be in the know:

• Have access to your young person's password accounts.

• Inform your child/ loved one that you may check in on their social media sites

• There's nothing wrong with monitoring their texts on a weekly basis. Know what they're thinking/doing/contemplating

• Ensure that their accounts are not open for public access as well as turning off location settings which is an instant 'hi, I'm here' alerting predators to their placement and habits. Scary stuff!

• Chat with your kids about what constitutes being a friend on any social media site. Predators troll and can connect via friend of a friend of a friend = not a real friend and red flags should go up.

Social media even impacts our kids' sleeping habits. Set limits on what hours the phone is accessible. Quality of sleep is directly related to an interrupted sleep cycle. That means those 2:00 am texts and 4:00 am Twitter feeds. There is no middle of the night text or posting that can be justified. If it's an emergency, a phone call can be made. I believe that since our kids are neither the President or the Pope there's no reason for any social media action after 10 pm. Just my two cents. You can witness the impact every day in any hallway of any middle or high school across the country; it's crazy.

Our kids' brains are constantly in motion when the cell is a permanent fixture. The ability to communicate face to face and the rise in anxiety with the need for constant stimulation are two huge areas of impact on this generation. It's frightening, but it's not too late. I encourage you to hop on Twitter, scroll through your kid's Instagram and stay in a loop that is in sore need of monitoring. It's a crazy world, but a whole lot less scary when we have the ability to be our kid's wingman.

Human Trafficking

Ruminating on heavy and stomach churning issues isn't something we look forward to. A lot of the time it can be more comfortable to avoid, but there are certain realities that are so dark and twisted avoiding them can be catastrophic. One of those dark, dirty topics is human trafficking.

The first time I invited a speaker to share the realities and dangers of trafficking, selling and prostituting of other human beings it caused heads to turn and questions to be asked. Until recently there has been very little media focus on human trafficking and when it has been a focus, it was nearly always an international issue. Human trafficking is very real, frightening and it is an issue in every state of America and throughout Europe, Asia and beyond. Educating our young people, their parents and those within our community on what it looks like and how to prevent it is critical. I believe education on this topic can save lives. Our kids (age appropriate, of course) need to hear what is going on and how social media plays a massive role in young people falling prey to perpetrators.

My speaker, Kelly Master the founder of Dining for Dignity, had less than an hour to condense a message that she was on fire about. Her eyes had witnessed survivors of human trafficking attempting to reclaim dignity and return to a state of normalcy. Her ears had listened to stories of young boys and girls lured into (what was assumed to be an informal, fun meet up) prostitution through promises of fame or love via social media only to be drugged up and pimped out on the streets for sex. How do you squish all of that passion into fifty minutes? This is a message that is uncomfortable, but one that kids, parents, neighbors and community members need to hear.

Not until recently has there been much in the way of public outcry about the stark reality of trafficking human lives for sex. It was something that was in the far corners of our minds that was far removed from our communities, because one would only assume it was an atrocity occurring in less 'civilized' communities. Whatever that means. Thailand, Russia, Nigeria, etc., roll a little easier off the tongue than New Jersey, California, Iowa and North Carolina. It is here and our loved ones are at risk. We can no longer turn a blind eye.

This is where our eyes have to be open. Our ears need to be acutely tuned in. Social media needs to be monitored with our kids. We must educate not only ourselves, but our kids. Strangers preying on those they hope to lure in through social media "friending" on Instagram, Tinder, etc. under false pretense. But who is really behind that screen? With all the crazy around us, there is a naivety among our young people prone to trust that how their new 'friend' depicts themselves is accurate. Why wouldn't it be?

Am I freaking you out? Good. We are in a war that consists of too many idle players. Humans are being sold like you would buy an object at Costco. Children, teenagers and women (and some men) are being sold for sex. Their bodies viewed as property. Their pimp controls where they eat, sleep and breathe, technically they own them. They control who pays for and receives sex. Where is the outcry? Where is the battle gear? Our speaker, Kelly Master, the founder of Dining for Dignity, is an inspiring, on fire red head that is fighting a dark, evil battle to reclaim lives.

It's learning that we must constantly remind our kids that unless you know the individual you shouldn't be communicating with them via social media or text. I think it's hard to imagine that nice couple who comes in for breakfast every Saturday chatting to their waitress as having the potential of being a tag team of pimps aiming to lure vulnerable prey into their circle. Or to consider that talent scout who reaches out to you and your child with glowing prospects of fame and fortune as being a twisted deviant wanting nothing more than to profit off of selling naked pictures of your child, getting her or him drugged up and prostituted out for cash. Heavy crap. Twisted stuff. It makes my skin crawl and makes me sick, but it is happening and we can no longer keep our eyes closed and our ears shut. Ignorance is ridiculously scary in these situations. Remain aware, chat with the young people in your life and just keep communicating.

It's a battle that can be fought even in the smallest of ways, but every step begins with awareness. What does human trafficking look like? What are some signs of someone who is being held against his/her will? The following information was obtained from the Polaris Project, an awesome website. Empowerment and change can happen when we become educated about topics that are impacting the innocent.

What to look for:

• Physical appearance: looking unkempt, malnourished

• Mental health/behavior: skittish, consistently on edge or nervous, overwhelming sadness or depression, noticeably defensive or paranoid when chatting about family history or law enforcement, not able to have consistent stories.

• Family history: where they live/lived can be patchy, lacking a real timeline and can seem to be rehearsed when recounting.

• Detachment from those around them (colleagues, students, peers, etc.) No independence. No personal space.

• Their daily activities are monitored in where they are at all times.

• Personal documentations are held onto by someone else (ID, passport, etc.).

• They are very point "A to B", attending work or school and nothing else.

• Lacking personal possessions, nothing is really their own.

• Actions and opinion overseen by someone else – they have no voice.

• They are monitored or lacking control of their finances, bank account. There are also signs and red flags of what to look for in someone who is being human trafficked or used as a sex slave.

Signs indicating someone may be being held against their will:

• Not able to go anywhere without permission.

• They have a pimp or a manager and are working in the sex industry.

• There is excessive debt they can't break free from.

• They work long hours, but pay is minuscule.

• Hours for work are exceptionally long and pay is either nonexistent or minimal.

• Breaks are not allowed or restrictions at work are unusual.

• Work place or home is out of the norm with security measures (cameras) or limited views (windows boarded or taped up).

Let your voice be heard. Keep your eyes open. Know that your efforts, words and insight could not only protect your loved ones, but also save an innocent heart from a pain no one deserves.

If you have suspicions or you have a nagging gut feeling that something is off, you have every right to make a phone call to your local authorities. Call, reach out and express your concerns. If you're wrong, there is no consequence. If you're right, you just freed a human being from a living hell. Your voice means something. I believe if we open our eyes and educate others the tide can and will turn. We can do this.

If you have suspicions that someone is a victim of human trafficking please contact the **National Human Trafficking Hotline: 888.373.7888**

Misconstrued Messages of Candy and Tart Hearts

It's not always easy to keep things in perspective. We get a myriad of mixed messages about self-worth and love from social media and a culture that is pretty whack a doodle. These mixed messages can make it difficult to focus on others as well as providing an inauthentic definition of self-love and what it means to be loved.

Valentine's Day has never been a holiday that I've looked forward to or really found much to it outside of the pressure for purchasing chocolates, roses or twirling around like Buddy the Elf chanting, *"I'm in love! I'm in love!"* I've always felt, in a non-jaded way, that the message conveyed by our culture is you lack value if you don't have a significant other and if you do you would only naturally expect to be laden with chocolates, flowers and uber love. So maybe that makes me sound cynical or anti-affectionate, but I personally feel that love and caring for others stretches way beyond what society has packaged and molded it into. Love is a pretty rad, beautiful thing.

Love is beautiful, unconditional and hard work. It's not earned in a one-night stand. With friendship it isn't solidified in a forty-eight hour meet and greet session. Unfortunately, we're in a culture where our food, internet service and expectations for everything and anything are immediate with the push of a button. It's easy to be impatient, to want something now and for it to unrealistically fall under our umbrella of what love and relationships should be even if they aren't.

One of my favorite verses in the Bible defines what love is so eloquently and so against the grain of what our society and culture defines it as:

1 Corinthians 13:4-7 (NIV)

4 Love is patient, love is kind. It does not envy. It does not boast. It is not proud. 5. It does not dishonor others. It is not self-seeking. It is not easily angered. It keeps no record of wrongs. 6 Love does not delight in evil, but rejoices with the truth. 7 It always protects, always trusts, always hopes, always perseveres.

Love is not an easily packaged, cellophane wrapped gift basket, but it is ever growing and developing. It isn't intended to hurt or weaken, but instead find ways to bring joy and fulfillment to another in the most non self-serving way.

There's nothing wrong with chocolates and a nice dinner on February 14th, but don't allow these notions of affection to be limited to a few designated holidays during the three hundred and sixty-five day calendar year. You deserve goodness, to be genuinely asked how your day was and to be surrounded by those (even if that's only a select few) who treat you how you deserve to be treated. Life is too short to invest and strive for a certain someone who will never reciprocate and treat you as you deserve to be treated.

Know that you, with all your good, bad and in-between are super worth loving and investing in. It's the truth! Don't settle....ever!

Fertummelt

There are poignant moments in life when we realize that we're not in a good place and change needs to happen. It may be an overwhelming sense of emptiness that material objects cannot fill, feelings of angst that may be triggered by either an individual or situation or the discontentment with your family dynamics; there is a feeling of discontentment and yearning to change gears.

When we're not in a good place, we can either do something about it or not. Depending on the situation, it may not be so simple, but help can't really ever successfully be a forced thing. There has to be a little give on the recipient's end.

The truth is most of us are stubborn. Some openly flock to tweaking and adjusting to get themselves in a healthier place, but I'd say they're the minority. In my past fourteen years in the mental health field I'm always intrigued by how many young people or adults will express how unhappy they are with how they are feeling, how life is going for them or the ongoing desire to change the direction they are heading in. They vent, unload and many times will just sit and stare waiting for an answer. Sometimes I'm given a, *"so what should I do?"* or a *"how can I stop feeling this way?"* There have been many times that I've already given half a dozen or more tips and strategies that went unheard simply because they were not listening, but that's OK.

It's not fun to feel out of control or in a place where we are unsatisfied with how life is going. There is no automatic switch to be flipped on to feel a sense of happiness or contentment, but in order for that to be a possibility it requires a game plan. Re-adjusting consists of taking the initial step of admitting you want to feel differently and the willingness to map out a bit of a plan consisting of changing certain habits, reaching out to others and considering personal counseling. These are just a few small steps, but it's fascinating how many choose to unload, but go no further. Whether its fear or uncertainty there is something that holds them back and so the rut or discontentment continues. Many times we meet up again weeks, months or even years later and it's apparent who has made the decision for self-help and those who have continued to delay it. Bottom line, there are many routes to getting things re-adjusted, it's being willing to take that step and be open to what your options are.

Thoughts from a few graduates who decided to make change go from thought to action:

"I feel as though every day I get a little better or I make a decision that I would not have made if I did not receive the help I got in high school. My time spent in Drug Squad and personal counseling...changed my life. I have become more confident and learned to overcome. That being said I still have baggage I carry with me from my father. I probably always will, but I feel as time goes on I learn how not to let it weigh me down. I am now going into my senior year of college, in a very healthy relationship with a wonderful girl, I'm very close with my mom, sister, and grandfather, and I'm just living life even with my upbringing being less than ideal."

"I think everyone goes through struggles and these unite us. I wouldn't call it circumstances either. We are just victims of the pitfalls of life. To quote Forest Gump,
"Life's like a box of chocolates, you never know what you're going to get." We all face strife and I think that's what really helped me. Knowing that I'm not alone in struggling truly allowed me to heal."

"I try to lead by my example. In past I was into LSD and mushrooms, but I was able to put those things down and see the beauty of the world and life for myself. I try to lead a healthy life. I try to show others that you can love the life you're given regardless of how challenging your upbringing may have been."

There will always be plenty of time to make excuses, but change and progress requires taking that first step. You can do it!

The Drug Squad is a peer prevention program I created in 2005 that is focused on building relationships, empowerment and cultivating positive peer pressure among student members. The mantra veers from the common slogans such as, *"don't do drugs."* Instead, we roll with *"make good decisions"*. It's essentially kids empowering kids through sharing their own struggles and challenges conveying that there is so much more to life than substances. The message involves self- care, empowerment and living life as fully as possible.

We're Onions, Baby!

You have Spanish onions; you have your Vidalia, Sweet, Shallots, White and a heap more. The outside seems predictable, but the inside; well every single onions interior is different. It just is. Every one of us has layers due to the circumstances and experiences that we have had in life. Some have more layers than others or thicker exteriors. Very few wear their layers on their sleeve. You have no concept of what that person has been through and it may be so easy to dismiss them due to their appearance, accent, demeanor, etc.

Be kind to others. You don't have to like everyone, but being mean, judgmental or making unfounded assumptions isn't fair. It attributes to some of the anger, stereotyping and discomfort we have simply because we judge. All of us do it to one capacity or another, but I challenge you to take some time and begin listening before assuming. I urge you to give someone you think you might know before you know them a chance. Just give it a go.

The kids I have worked with over the years have been my greatest teachers in learning the concept of the onion. Every kid, each heart holds something different. I have felt like such a butt head when I've been too quick to make an assumption about a kid whether that's due to appearance, family history, or just the word on the street about that person. How unfair is it of me to reinforce something that kid is already facing every day by peers and society? I've learned so much from kids who knock my socks off continuing to teach, inspire and challenge me to grow.

I'd like to share some thoughts from graduates who externally looked like they had it together in high school, but internally were falling apart. They simply needed to be heard, loved and encouraged.

Words from a few graduates:

"The loneliest and most challenging period of my life was during my sophomore year of high school. A close family member had overdosed, and was in rehab, and my world was falling apart at the seams. I felt like I couldn't tell anyone. At this point I was dealing with daily or multiple times a day panic and anxiety attacks and depression. I felt alone and incapable of lifting myself out of the pit of despair. I pulled away from my friends, I didn't talk, and I could feel myself drifting away."

"For the first two years of my high school experience, I felt pretty alone with my home life. I felt like I couldn't tell anyone, and if I did, they would judge me or not be able to relate to me. I didn't even tell my best friends about what was happening at home."

"The loneliness time in my life was eighth grade. No one could even try to understand my situation. I feel like no one could help."

"My biggest fear in high school was being exposed. On the exterior, I had it all together. I was on the Varsity Cheerleading Squad. I was taking AP classes and had friends in pretty much every social group. I always had a guy that I liked. You could say I had it all. But when I went home, that wasn't quite the case."

"I didn't really like to relate to others, I felt that I wanted to be different and I wanted my pain to be the only thing that set me apart from others. I was very twisted in my teen years after the loss of my older sister. I sought pain before anything else. And I wanted to feel that pain by myself."

Chewy Didn't Roll Solo

Goose had *Maverick* and *Han Solo* had *Chewbacca*. Both of these guys had a wingman through the course of their journeys that endured both the good and bad. With each chapter in life we need our own Chewy or Goose, but our kids need a wingman.

Whether it be in the hallways of their high schools or on the weekends, every young person will be faced with decisions, moral dilemmas and peer pressures that can often be uncomfortable and sometimes has the potential to be life altering. It's that person who not only has your back, but will call you out on poor decision making or will stand up for you when you are in over your head. Often times it takes a handful of experiences involving hurt, broken promises or even betrayal before the selection process becomes more refined. It isn't an easy thing.

After completing grad school I spent six months working in New Zealand and a few weeks traveling throughout Australia and Fiji. While in Fiji, I island-hopped in pursuit of good surf and diving. I met some locals who owned a dive shop on the main land and they invited me to do a trek with them free of charge. I was a very green diver, only receiving my cert a month or so earlier in Australia with only a handful of dives under my belt. When you dive you're always supposed to have a buddy, or a wingman. My wingman, Raj, assured me that I was in good hands and that we were going to check out an unbelievable wreck that had sunk a few hundred years back. I wasn't wreck dive certified, but I caved in, put on my gear and eagerly accompanied my wingman into the deep blue.

As we descended I kept my eyes fixed on Raj who would turn around every ten feet or so bobbing his head and flashing a thumbs up. I slowly followed him through the first passageway into the ship and as we entered visibility quickly decreased and my wingman was out of sight. There would be different doorways to go through and it was unclear as to which way they turned making it a very real possibility of getting lost in the belly of the ship. I knew the others were probably only a few feet ahead, but I opted to make my way back to the surface. But as I hastily exited the doorway the knob on my air tank became pinned in between the rusty shards of the door's frame. I couldn't move forward or backwards and for a second I was pretty sure that I was done for. The only option remaining was in removing my weight belt and physically holding my air tank as I maneuvered my body and was facing my tank. I jostled it and after a few jiggles the knob was free and I was able to strap my gear back on and resurface.

My wingman did not have my back. I remember thinking on the boat ride back to land how differently my outcome could have been. My ability to trust someone I knew nothing about was foolish on my part. How incredibly naïve was I to entrust my life in the hands of a complete stranger? Impulsivity and foolishness could have had led to a very different outcome.

Every day adults and teens are faced with situations that have the potential to be life altering. These range from whether or not to say something if you're in the car and the driver's texting, to speaking up when you overhear someone being bullied, to posting inappropriate comments/pictures on social media and the list goes on. Sometimes we have our guard down, aren't thinking straight or are just simply being a butt head. It's times such as these that we need to be held accountable, be called out and need a wingman.

Life is simply too short not to have a wingman.

Words from graduates...

"I self harmed for about six months. I never wanted to reach out to anyone until Lawler came until my life. She truly allowed me to realize I was worth more than I believed; that I was worth more than I believed and that I had potential and that my life events didn't define me. I wouldn't have reached out for help if it wasn't for her. I really don't know what would have happened if she didn't reach out to me. She allowed me to break free from this low point and truly blossom."

"The loneliest point in my life was in the eighth grade. No one around me could even understand my situation. I felt no one could help me. All of my friends and I were depressed for one reason or another and we would just be depressed together. When we were apart we would cut ourselves with anything we could. I could hardly bare the physical pain like cutting and I found myself not eating and thriving off of the pain. It reminded me that I was alive and the pain soon became comforting. It's a battle I still fight to this day. I found myself getting better when I became part of the Drug Squad. Being involved in the Drug Squad and starting to go to counseling changed my life."

Emotional Bingo

Even in this day and age when I mention or recommend counseling, whether with a teenager or an adult, there is a pause, rolling of the eyes (most of the time inadvertently) or a perception that chatting with a 'shrink' (yup, still a reference that floats out there) is not their thing. I have to admit, even while I was in grad school training to be a counselor I was all about helping others, but didn't deem it applicable for myself. I was stubborn and I convinced myself that counseling was for people who couldn't handle life without someone throwing them a rope to reel them in and it mental health field. I'm here to say I was wrong. The first step, after all, is acceptance, isn't it?

I know not everyone is keen on chatting with a stranger. But give me a few minutes of your time. The perks of sorting things out in your head, gaining some insight and picking up some tools that can be applied to everyday life is that you don't bump into that person in your kitchen and they aren't sitting in the cubby next to you at work. There's also the perk of having a third party, neutral person involved who can shed light and insight in ways most of us cannot accomplish when we're in the middle of it all.

With what the average person contends with each day and then throwing in a crisis, chemical imbalance or the simple fact of being a teenager, counseling can really assist in an individual getting on the right track. It isn't intended to be a magical two session cure. I will interject that it is human nature to have limited patience combined with unrealistic expectations: *I've been angry for twenty-three years and why is it after five sessions I'm still angry?* Hmmm…let me think. It takes time!!! If your kids have been subjected to a life time of mom and dad living in a toxic relationship, a young man who has struggled with severe anxiety, the brother who lost his older sibling or the neighbor who has witnessed his wife struggle with depression while trying to kick her pill habit, everything takes time, patience and a willingness to change. If there is a lack of willingness and desire to gain insight and clear out the mind the likelihood of anything progressive happening is as limited as it gets.

Be your own advocate. If you opt for counseling then go in with a list of what you want to work on. Be open to the change that the person you are sitting in session with might call you out on. A good counselor will push your buttons, make you uncomfortable and dig up feelings you may have never allowed yourself to experience before. There will be moments of discomfort; that's a good thing. Change requires reflection. Reflection can be super uncomfortable, but without willingness to look at your heart and mind, there's zero chance of something positive coming out of a session that is costing both time and money.

It's easier to talk about wanting to change and have visions of how you would like to see yourself. When the transition from talk to action occurs it can become uncomfortable territory. 'Cleaning house' isn't usually overly awesome. Looking at ourselves in the mirror can be uncomfortable when you don't like what is staring back at you. It takes time. But the longer we postpone sorting out who we are, the more cluttered and skewed our perception of who we are becomes.

On the other hand, I also know that not all Counselors were really meant to be Counselors. There are also those mental health professions whose ability to connect and be effective has been effected after years of professional weariness. Their hearts are tired and burnt out. Others can bring in their personal rubbish. I've heard some awful stories from the counselor who clipped their toenails during a session, to chatting about their own struggle with weight loss or even the one who would nod in and out of consciousness. There are crappy counselors out there, just like there are subpar mechanics, dentists, plumbers and lawyers. You have to advocate for yourself and whether it's through recommendations of a friend, relative, associate or your doctor names can be thrown in the mix of good, bad and in between.

But remember, you have to be patient. I equate finding the right fit with a counselor to going shopping for a pair of jeans. I really do not enjoy shopping for jeans. It's not anywhere near the top of my list of things I enjoy doing. It forces me to look at myself in the most non-flattering, skewed dimensional dressing room mirror. I'm reluctant, but I put myself through the fitting process because I'm all about jeans. When you find that perfect pair of jeans, it's all worth it. I love jeans. I live in them and will probably be buried in them. But just like the frustrating, annoying jean fitting process it's the same deal with a counselor. Sometimes the first try is a fit. Sometimes it isn't. Remember, just like there are boot cut, flare, low rise and high rise fits of those trusty jeans it's the same with counselors. It's OK to ask what their background is and it's OK to ask friends about their experiences or recommendations. Be your own advocate, research and find that pair of jeans that fits best for you.

I tell kids I work with that if they aren't comfortable chatting with me there's their guidance counselor, parent, uncle, aunt or older sibling. Not everyone that sits on my comfy, worn blue couch is going to feel the 'fit' with me. I get it. I don't take it personally. The important thing is that they make it a priority to seek out that someone who fits and that it's someone who knows what they're talking about. Many think they do, the numbers drop when it comes down to the fact that they don't.

I do recommend counseling. I think it can do awesome, life altering things. But I do realize it isn't for everyone. A thought I have is, that you should give it a go a few times, be opened minded and see if the fit happens. I realize it's expensive, sometimes very expensive. Often, insurance companies can recommend counselors who are in network for a limited number of sessions in your area. Compare that list with someone you know and trust. Selecting a name by closing your eyes and pointing is more likely than not to end up not having a good outcome. Take your time, ask questions and see what feedback you get from people.

Even if it's five or six sessions that are approved, it's something. There are county and state programs that offer pro-rated, sliding scale counseling options through the department of mental health services. Contact your local agency. Feel free to request for a male or female counselor or one who specializes in a certain area. My plea is, if you take the step, allow yourself to be open-minded. I have witnessed so many go in reluctant, cynical and guarded only to validate their perception of counseling after a few ineffective sessions. It's sort of like trying to navigate your way through your favorite store with your hands over your eyes and earplugs in your ears. You're going to get around a little bit, but not really make any progress in your shopping ventures and at the end of it you're just super frustrated. It's a counteractive approach that just doesn't benefit anyone.

The truth is that not everyone has the means to go to counseling. There are also individuals who will never step foot in a counselor's office. What still remains important is finding that someone to vent, lighten the laundry load and also organize your thoughts. Certainly not everyone fits the bill for listening, discernment and insight. There are some really poor listeners and those who are so not equipped to give their insight. Be selective. Take your time in finding a pulse on someone who you care for and respect and pick their brain. But it is wise to be selective and advantageous to take your time.

Nationwide, free 24-7 anonymous hotline numbers provide an ear for those young and old. In the South Jersey area we have 2nd Floor and Contact, two wonderful services that offer up advice and an ear to anyone at any time. The good thing is that it's as judge free as it gets while dealing with people who have been trained to guide and chat in a constructive helping way. Now, how can you beat that?

Getting in touch with who you are is important. The first time I said that out loud to a student I thought it sounded very counselor cliché, but it's true. The longer I'm in the field the greater respect I have for taking the time to figure out who we are, allocating time to seek wisdom from those we trust and making ourselves more of a priority. If we are clueless on what makes us tick and our overall plusses and minuses, how can we realistically expect to have a healthy take on life and to maintain healthy relationships? We can't. It's impossible. If you don't get 'you' and it's something you'd rather not take the time to focus on it's impossible to be able to maintain any authentic, healthy relationships. If you don't know who you are, how the heck is anyone else going to have a shot at tackling that one?

A few years ago I was at a workshop for addiction counselors. There were a ton of vendors selling books, games, etc., for us to bring back to our schools and utilize with our kids. My friend suggested Emotional Bingo. I'll admit it, I laughed. My response to the quirky little sketched characters on the front of the box with a few dozen different emotional facial expressions was nothing short of it being totally lame. There was no way my kids were going to go for that. After all, they're in high school and are pretty quick to judge anything that just validates their already skittish view of counseling. Now, I was going to have a four by four poster game board with little emotional characters encouraging putting it all on the line. I bought it.... hook, line and sinker.

The funny thing is that it works. Do the kids cheer when the game board makes its way out of my filing cabinet? No, but as we sit, throw the dice and give it a whirl it's funny how into it they are. Why? Most of us are uncomfortable delving into our feelings. It may feel awkward. We don't really make the time to think about the emotions connected to certain people in our lives, experiences in past and present and how we view ourselves. Yes, judge me for sounding like a super sappy counselor. The truth is that when these kids are crouched on my office floor taking the forty-two minutes to connect their present with identifying what makes them mad, anxious, jealous and sad it's really pretty cool. We all feel. Each of us has our own set of emotions. It's just taking the time to figure out what it is that makes us tick. The dissecting of what makes us tick isn't easy, but it's really pretty rewarding.

I love when I have a student who will connect the dots and realize how overwhelmingly anxious he/she is about getting enough hours in at work to pay car insurance, how angry he is at a parent who drinks too much (something they have no control over), to the sadness that seems to be squelching all joy from their lives about the break up with their boyfriend or girlfriend. There are some things that we have control of and some we do not. We cannot change the people around us. We only have control of our own emotions, decisions and outlook on life. Emotional Bingo is what we choose to play each day of our lives.

It is our choice whether we allow ourselves to know what we feel and how we feel about it. It's the choice of walking around with our eyes closed and denying that life is happening and pretending that we don't need to really think about it. When we walk around with closed eyes, our natural response is to put our hands out and grapple. We fumble. We bump into things; things that are so obviously in front of us it's as plain as day. But our eyes are closed. It causes us to make turns in directions we would never take if we just simply opened our eyes. It has a tendency to lead us into people, places and things that are typically not in our best interest.

My Dad is an alcoholic. My brother and I can hardly make eye contact never mind maintain a conversation without an argument erupting. We used to get along, but now I just think we're so busy with our own lives and communicating is something we're both pretty crap at. But I know we need each other. I'm at that point now. I think I'm tired of letting Dad's sickness beat the crap out of me. I think I can't fight something that I can't control. I need to figure me out. Being angry and sad all the time isn't making anything any better. Me smoking my face off all the time isn't fixing it either. It used to relax me. Now, weed is what I think I have been using a crutch to just not deal with what I need to. That's wild to think I even thought that maybe that would make it better. But it's time to change. I'm freaking out how scared I am, but I won't become Dad. I won't end up alone, barely paying the bills, hated by my kids. I won't let myself become what he is. So I'm going to do this. I can do this. I will do this. Life will not kick my ass. Today is the beginning of a new day.

Keeping our eyes open gaining a sense of where we are (no matter how scary and overwhelming the situation may be) is how life was intended to be experienced. Maintaining a sense of reality isn't always an easy thing. It's allowing yourself to feel the sadness in your heart when you've lost someone you cared so desperately about or acknowledging the anger you have towards the relative who is once again off the wagon causing further stress on family members. Or there's the anxiety you have with that coworker who makes the eight hour work day all the more awful than it already is. How we feel about things is important. Connecting our emotions with different people, varying situations is something we need to do, but rarely take the time to do.

The significance in all this is sorting out how we feel, figuring out what and who triggers these (good/bad) emotions. This lays the groundwork for taking the next BIG step in realizing that we're in charge of how we feel. Yes, I'm using emotions again. What we are not in charge of (something that is really, really hard to wrap our brains around) is changing other people. We spend WAY too much time on that. No one is responsible for how you feel other than you. No one is responsible for what you do other than you. When we grasp that, it's then the choice to allow negative, life consuming emotions to cripple us or we can open our eyes and push forward in ways that allow us to really live.

You may not be able to change the world, but we can change ourselves, and that, my friend, has the ability to have a ripple effect that can stretch beyond your comprehension.

Thoughts from a graduate:

"My struggles have moved with me more than I have moved from them, but that's only because I use them to do positive in this world. Through the Drug Squad I spoke of my issues to show people with similar struggles that they weren't alone. To show them that you don't have to let your past have negative effects on your future. I have brought that mindset with me to my career and adult life today. My struggle as a child made me a better man today and a better Marine."

Windshield & Rear View

It's not only our personal decision to take ownership of our emotions, but it's up to us as to whether we decide to live in the past or stay in the present. Each of us has a story. Each one of us is our own novel with pages, chapters and experiences that the majority we encounter through life will never know about. Every word and page is our own and we are the keepers of the story. It is up to us as to who and when certain parts of our novel are revealed. There are those who will choose to divulge very little and others who will keep the pages more accessible than most.

The one commonality is that we have our own covers. We all look very different in size, color and demeanor but our outer exterior is what it is. Some covers are a little more worn and weathered while others have maintained their original condition. Life sometimes has a way of wearing you down.

Each of us has our own memories, hurts and joys as well as chapters that really make us who we are. Some novels are deeper than others. Some novels are longer than others whether that is due to life experience or the time they were given here on earth. The reality is that not one novel on the face of the planet is the same. We, like books and snowflakes, are all unique. Once we realize our uniqueness it makes us less inclined to compare ourselves to the outer covers and the chapters of others around us.

One of our greatest vices as humans is our past. Whether it's in chapter one of our life or chapter twenty -two, the past can be one of the greatest challenges to overcome. Our past is a part of us, but it does not have to dictate the individual we become. That is easier said than done. It might be trust issues connected to our mom who chose her newest boyfriend over you. Or the anger that rears it's irrational head in arguments that stem from the hurt you experienced time and time again from someone you trusted. It could be the crippling sense of sadness that encompasses you during the holidays as yet another reminder that the one you love is no longer here. Experiences and memories that are part of who we are, but can have a tremendous impact on the path that we take in our lives.

We are very simple but complex beings. Each of our stories are part of who we are, but the challenge we all will face (whether we acknowledge it or not) is to allow our past to be a part of who we are OR to have it dictate who we are and who we will become. Our pains, disappointments, joys and trials are ingredients for each of us as individuals. But the giant mother ship of an obstacle will be whether we live in the now or the then.

It's like when you drive a car. My hope would be that both hands are on the wheel and all focus is on the road. Let's go with that one. When we drive we do get distracted. In order to drive our vehicle we have to look ahead through the windshield, glancing occasionally at the rear view mirrors. We glance to see what's on our side and what's behind us. But we only take the occasional glance.

What we pass along our drive in life and what is behind us can become a struggle to not become fixated upon. We can also choose to blame ourselves for or possess an innate fear of becoming what we have witnessed in our past. Different chapters or events in our lives can sometimes become our greatest enemy. Being bound by what was, what could have been and what should have been disallows the ability to live fully in the present and cuts us off at the ankles in our progression towards the future.

You're in the driver's seat. What happens if you just focus on what's ahead of you? All focus is and remains on what is in front of the windshield. Looking ahead, slowing down when needed and staying in a state of constant movement is good. It's good, but not the best. Now what occurs if all attention is turned to the rear view mirror? The plus is you can see if anyone is approaching you, the vehicles behind you and possibly scattered road kill and potholes that you managed to avoid. The inevitable outcome of the rear view focus is a crash. You will, one hundred percent, ram into another car, smash into a guardrail or veer off the road going into something or someone. It's a given.

The past, or our rear view mirror, is an important part of our lives and of driving. But relying solely on what lies behind us is dangerous. It is bound for disaster. Nothing good comes from focusing and wrestling with something that you cannot go back and change. There is no jug handle in the past. There is no k-turn to re-do. Trying to live in a "would have, could have" way of life is de-habilitating.

Living in the past comes in all different shapes and sizes. It's the kid I bump into who graduated seven years prior with no real direction in life, sort of floundering and every conversation begins with how life was while in high school. The chat never reaches beyond seven years ago with a life freeze framed with scoring goals, dating reflections and parties. Or it's the now late twenty to thirty year olds who are working their minimum wage jobs, no real aspirations for college or trade school and spend their nights playing beer pong in their high school friend's garage before smoking up to Zeppelin and chasing it with a bag of Doritos. The middle aged man who, forty years ago, used to work on jets in the Air Force. Now, there is rarely an hour that lapses where what was is not a topic of the conversation. It's all what used to be. Nothing spans beyond what would be deemed as their peak chapter in life.

Some small town and in some small city
there's an unattended heart
with a distorted view of the past tangled
with an inhibited outlook
of the future
conversations laden with what was,
what could have been
and what should have been
the pause button of life has taken its grip
and stepping into the next frame is not an option.
Or so they think.
Football passes.
Boyfriend with his motorcycle.
Bonfires and shin-digs of past.
Let it go. It is part of you, may it not define you.
May it not dictate conversations.
A chapter in a life with so much awaiting.
The choice will be theirs. The choice is their own.

Another more heart wrenching rear view mirror approach is the personal losses that flip everything upside down. It's the mom unable to put up a Christmas tree for the past ten years because it's too much of a reminder of the daughter who is no longer here. It is the child who is emotionally detached from everyone after years of a father who left and returned so many times she can't count; every time promising he would do better. The sixteen year old who has a bong stashed under his bed that he lights up every night to keep the flashes of what happened to him ten years ago from surfacing in his dreams. So many of us can feel trapped and controlled by what was.

The past can have a strong hold that can feel like steel chains on our hands and feet. We become prisoners of our past that can have immeasurable implications on the decisions we make, the road we travel and the mentality we assume throughout our lifetime. But breaking free and allowing yourself to live again is not a 1,2,3 process. It takes time, persistence and maybe a tissue box or two. It is one day, one week and one step at a time. With the shackles of what was there is no legitimate fast forward button to go beyond having to take a look at the hurt and then move onward. It's not so simple.

For that individual living in what was back in high school, college, etc. it's about finding contentment in the now. Going beyond the highlights of the past and investing in tangible goals and stages that can create momentum for good things to happen and having something to look forward to. There isn't anything wrong with reflecting every now and again on the past highlights or low lights of our past chapters. It's just making sure that it's not a pattern and does not hinder stepping forward.

To those with aching hearts and heavy minds I am sorry for the weight you bear. What I can say is that harboring devastating sadness or even hatred towards those who have hurt you deeply and the gash you bear can seem to pulsate. It can feel like these emotions are streaming through your veins. Hatred, anger and loathing of those who have hurt you festers and can transform into bitterness. The road from anger to bitterness is a transition that happens over time and can, just like cancer, take over and destroy. Loss, hurt and disappointment can shatter the heart but it is something that those who endure it have to make the conscious decision of whether or not to forge ahead. But that timeline is dependent on the person, circumstance and timing.

One of the most devastating aspect of hurt, loss and grief is the surfacing of bitterness. I believe it can destroy hearts and lives. I have witnessed so many choose the road to bitterness and I can tell you that it can take you down. My feeling is that it is our decision, albeit one of the most gut wrenching, to let go and move forward and to refuse to be a victim. It is allowing yourself to survive. It is not allowing a disease, a circumstance or another human being to emotionally enslave you where it has now claimed another victim. It just wouldn't be fair.

I'm not pleading with you as anything other than someone who at one time couldn't look myself in the mirror without questioning the reflection staring back at me. I was almost a victim of bitterness, but instead I am a survivor.

In the spring of 1999 I was a junior in college at the University of North Carolina. I had plans to attend Oxford University in the summer and my two sisters, Jess and Shana, planned on joining me in England where we would spend four weeks backpacking together through Europe. My sisters and I were always pretty close and this was something the three of us were so excited to experience together. It was going to knock off a number of goals on our bucket list.

On April 6, 1999, a little before noon in Kill Devil Hills, N.C. my sister, Shana, and her four friends Angie, Amanda, Megan and Mike were struck by a drunk driver. They were the third car that went through the intersection. They were t-boned. The driver made no attempt to stop and hit them at sixty-five mph. Angie and Amanda were killed on impact. Megan passed away on the way to the hospital. Mike, in the passenger seat, was the only survivor. Shana was ejected from the back and was flown to Norfolk Hospital. She held on for six days. Her injuries were too severe and she passed away on April 12. For six days it felt like the world stopped. Everything around me seemed to be spinning out of control and was one big blur all wrapped up into one. From the moment I learned of the crash, attended three funerals and followed it up with Shana passing; it was a mind-numbing week that has been seared into its very own chapter of my life.

Four beautiful, amazing lives snuffed out of this world because of one selfish decision. It's insane to think that one decision, one split second in time altered so many lives. Five families had the wind knocked out of them and there are days, even now years later, we still experience those moments where we miss our loved one so much it hurts to breathe.

I remember walking into the courtroom the day the trial of the state of North Carolina vs. Melissa Marvin began. My Dad, a pillar of strength and insight, said, *"Er, you have no idea of what lies behind these court room doors. You're going to hear things you can't prepare yourself for. You're going to have a choice to get angry and bitter. Don't let her win. Ask God for strength, comfort....please don't do this alone."* I knew he was right. I was scared to death of what lie ahead of us, but my pride and fury over rode all logic. I shut him out and for that I am so very sorry. I made my own decision driven by stubbornness and lack of understanding. He knew what was ahead and I had no concept until it was too late.

Lawyers went back and forth about the details of that day. For six days we learned of Melissa Marvin's past and present. Every moment of April 6th was broken down into a million seconds. We heard of the handful who encountered Melissa intoxicated and just let her get in her car and move to the next store and bar. They stayed silent. My heart was hardening. I was angry at the surf shop owner, the bar tenders, the bank teller and the others who chose silence over my sister's life. In my mind these people had the blood of four innocent girls on their hands. They were guilty through their silence.

EMTs and firefighters described what they witnessed upon arriving at the scene of the crash. Grown men held back tears all visibly impacted. Each witness reiterating that it was a level of devastation that they had never seen before. I heard things that I wish I hadn't. I visualized things that my mind wasn't prepared for. My heart hardened even further.

It was when Melissa Marvin spoke that the switch flipped. She didn't mean it. It was an accident. She couldn't bring them back; a million excuses without an ounce of sincerity. She wasn't remorseful, just sorry that she was caught and now her own life was inconvenienced. I could feel my heart hardening, but I also heard my father's words repeat over and over again. I knew I had a choice and it was mine to make. Even then in the courtroom I felt the tug in my heart to ask God for strength, truth and wisdom. But I closed the door and I allowed, right then and there, bitterness to begin rearing its ugly head.

I missed Shana more than air itself. I cried. I ached. But instead of grieving and beginning to allow my heart to mend I allowed bitterness to preside. I hated Melissa Marvin. I hated the people she came in contact with that day. I hated that I didn't have my sister anymore. I hated seeing people so happy when I wasn't. I hated that the world of five families had been flipped and shook around in a million different ways. I hated being alive.

For over two years I avoided grieving and just pushed my way through the motions of life. I wore a smile, but I kept a distance from almost everyone and did my best to ensure no one got into my heart. I drank a lot. Looking back now, alcohol was the last thing I should have been consoling my hurt with. But when you're emotionally unhinged, there's not a lot of logic swirling around. I had unhealthy relationships. I did everything to the extreme because even though I was scared of my own reflection I didn't feel like I had anything to loose.

I was wrapped up in my own hurt blind to the pain I was causing my own family. My parents witnessed me self-destructing in ways no one else ever knew. I pushed the envelope because I was miserable and they knew it and that drove me crazy. I didn't want to die, but I also didn't care about things that we are supposed to as humans. From surfing insanely out of my league waves, cliff jumping off the coast of Spain, sleeping in a tent in Greece with complete strangers to waking up and not remembering the night prior countless times because I yet again,

69

drank myself into a stupor. I was empty, lonely and numb. All I wanted was my sister back.

It was during a church service that my heart just couldn't take it anymore. I was sitting in the front pew, not by choice, but because I was late and that was always the last spot left. I hated sitting in the front. But as they began to sing a song that Jess and I walked Shana out to at her service my heart couldn't take it anymore. Tears welled up, my throat ached to the point that it was hard to breathe and I began to shake. I was like an emotional volcano on the brink of eruption and out of pride and sorrow, but I didn't want anyone to take notice.

I walked out of the service through the back door and crossed the bypass that led to the beach. It was there on the beaches of the Outer Banks, just two and a half miles from where the four crosses marking where the girls were killed stood, that I gave up. I was tired of fighting. I was tired of hating. I was tired of being tired. Melissa Marvin was destroying me and I couldn't do that to my parents, Jess and most of all Shana and the girls. I fell on my knees and I pled with God to forgive me for my hardened heart. Weeping, I asked for His forgiveness, mercy and that the only way I would ever survive the next chapters of my life was with Him directing me.

I was tired of walking around with an invisible backpack filled to the brim with bricks. The brick of anger, bitterness, loathing and resentment were so very heavy and I could no longer walk around each day with such a heavy load. I gave up. In that very instant I handed it all over to my Creator and Counselor. It was at that moment life was breathed back into me. My backpack was removed and for the first time in a very long time, I could breathe again.

There are still days many years after that afternoon that rocked our worlds to the core which are really a struggle. There are certain parts of my day or moments that make me think of Shana and I miss her with every fiber of my being. But I am

But I am not angry. I do not hate Melissa Marvin or her actions. I do believe she deserved her sentence of sixty years incarcerated for killing four people. I do believe if her sentence was the norm instead of the exception that there would be a decrease in people driving under the influence. I do believe that her actions caused a crash and not an accident. Accidents happen and they're not typically preventable whereas her actions had an inevitable domino effect, a ticking time bomb that crashed directly into the path of strangers. Her stranger was my best friend. Justice took place.

I've been asked if I ever think of Melissa Marvin or if I've forgiven her. My answer to the first question is that I don't allow myself to think about her. It is for no other reason than to not create an aching in my heart. Her decisions not only hurt our side of the equation, but her mom and family lost her as well. Just as her decisions set the outcome for the girls, it set her own outcome in motion as well. Sixty years behind bars is a lifetime void of really being able to live as her life was intended. In my heart, that seems only fair. But I do not hate her. I have forgiven her, but forgiveness does not equate to a lightening of justice.

Sadness is an inevitable part of life. But it is allowing grief or different levels of pain to be slowly released and to not become swallowed up with bitterness. It's a fight, a concerted effort that those part of the 'wounded hearts' club have to face. If it were not for my faith and my surrendering I'm not sure where I would be.

There are moments that my eyes shift from the windshield to the rear view mirror. I think of Shana often, but I do not allow myself to go any further than remembering the beauty of who she was and the seventeen years we had together. I know my limits. I look forward, eyes ahead, with the intention of living fully in a way that would make Shana proud. That is my present and that is my tomorrow.

The five families involved created the Precious Gems Memorial following the crash in memory of the girls. The focus of our organization, years later, continues to be urging young and old to know that driving under the influence and other destructive behaviors are just simply not worth it. There's power in good decision making.

Life's too short to be selfish.

Feel free to visit: www.preciousgemsmemorial.com

The Sixteen Year Old You

I have been privileged to work with many amazing hearts over the years. There have been so many kids that have impacted my heart in life altering ways. Throughout this book I've offered some of their thoughts and reflections. One of the questions I threw their way was, "If you could go back and give your sixteen year old self some words of wisdom, what would it be?" It's really cool to see how much of an impact a positive outlook on what is and was has had on you as a person.

What I would tell my sixteen-year old self:

"Your father does not define who you are or what you become. He is just a man who lost himself and it's sad because he's screwing himself, but there's nothing you can do to save him. He may love you and you may or may not love him, but he will just bring you down. You have to focus on yourself and the rest of your family because they love you more than you realize. They are a great source of inspiration. Focus on the future and I know when you're a father you'll only be the good parts of our father and not the bad."

"Be kind to your parents because everything they do is because they love you. Read your Bible more because you need it more than you can imagine. Get to know the people around you as well as you possibly can and love them even when it's hard. Also, five days after your sixteenth birthday is going to be the worst day of your life, but remember it's only a small blink in eternity."

" It's tough to think of what to say to your younger self when you are very happy with who and where you are in life. If anything, I'd use a quote you used to say to a lot of people: Keep on keeping on. For some reason that has stuck with me after all these years but yet it's so simple and powerful. Sure I wouldn't

make much of it but it's just one of those ways of saying it will all work out in the end. Some things are out of your control. Realize you are not the ultimate decider of your life. Take a deep breath, not everything is resting on your shoulders."

"I would tell my sixteen year old self to be safe and that there is always a new day ahead of you. The world is more than you think it is and all of it is within your fingertips."

"Looking back, I would tell my sixteen year old self that you are worth it. You are worth breaking up with that boy who treats you like crap. You are worth seeking help when you need it. You are worth surrounding yourself with people who lift you up instead of bring you down. I would tell my sixteen year old self that just because one man made a decision to pick up a beer, doesn't mean that you are any less of a person. You cannot control his addiction, but you can take control of whether or not you will make the same mistake. I would tell her that just because you were used to mental abuse for so long, you don't need to settle for that anymore. You are worth it."

What's Your Dash?

There is no rewind button in life. There is no ability to hit the pause button and readjust people, places and things to our liking. That would be pretty awesome, but it wasn't a button installed on our body anywhere from head to toe. So much of my appreciation of life has come from personal loss and standing in the trenches of the mental health field on a daily basis. Life is beautiful, although sometimes super painful. It very easily can make us bystanders.

But have you ever contemplated what you have done with your life? What if your last day on earth was today? I don't say that to freak you out, but if you knew your time was limited, would you change how you're living your every day? The truth is, our time is limited. Our life is but a vapor and so often we live as if we have forever, allowing days to slip by our fingertips without giving it a second thought. It's not living life in panic mode, but re-evaluating and contemplating your everyday and is it 'you' centered or 'others' centered?

I've read this poem a few times over the years to my kids and I think the message is clear and poignant:

THE DASH

I read of a man who stood to speak
at the funeral of a friend.
He referred to the dates on her tombstone,
from the beginning...to the end.
He noted that first came the date of her birth
and spoke of the following date with tears,
but he said what mattered most of all
was the dash between those years.
For that dash represents all the time
that she spent alive on earth
And now only those who loved her
know what that little line is worth.
For it matters not, how much we own,
the cars...the house...the cash.
What matters is how we live and love
and how we spend our dash.
So, think about this long and hard.
Are there things you'd like to change?
For you never know how much time is left
that can still be rearranged.
If we could just slow down enough
to consider what's true and real
and always try to understand
the way other people feel.
And be less quick to anger
and show appreciation more
and love the people in our lives
like we've never loved before.
If we treat each other with respect
and more often wear a smile,
remembering that this special dash
might only last a little while.
So, when your eulogy is being read,
with your life's actions to rehash...
would you be proud of the things they say
about how you spent YOUR dash?

Author – Linda Ellis

It's funny how we wake up, breathe in and out, do our daily tasks, fit in a few meals and conversations and somewhere in there we lapse into sleep only to do it all again the following day. Examining your life span shouldn't be perceived as something morbid or anxiety provoking. We are all going to hit the last act and scene of our individualized play at some point; there's no avoiding it. Once we become comfortable with that realization it has the potential to really alter the way our lives are conducted, what we do and do not focus on as well as maybe casting a shadow on how we spend our time and days.

In a society that is on the brink of fixation with both tragedy and disaster it seems ironic that most do their best to block out their own mortality. Click on the TV and there's not a five minute lapse in any local or national news program where someone somewhere has been abducted, robbed, shot at or killed. It's actually as predictable as it comes. I do my best to avoid watching the news or even reading different sections of the newspaper. Viewing thirty minutes of the past twenty -four hours of happenings in any surrounding community is typically laden with robbery, rape, abduction, shootings and overdose. After an eight- hour gig of every emotion under the sun it's really the last thing on my to do list.

But if you pause and take a few minutes to look around in today's world; there are a whole lot of people keeling over for a host of reasons. A quick stat is that every thirty seconds someone is killed in a car crash by someone under the influence. That's one hundred and twenty people in an hour and that's just the tip of the iceberg. The stark reality is that we're all at some point going to take our last breath and no longer exist. That truth doesn't scare me one bit. It drives me to run the race at a strong pace with every intention to make a difference, live with substance and to look forward not behind.

What occupation you hold, your social circle of friends and your involvement in the community might influence your exposure to loss or tragedy. Both living and working in a school district has probably skewed my perception of life and its fragility a bit. It seems nearly inevitable that in the course of a school year we will lose either a student or a graduate. It sucks. From texting and driving, drinking and driving, speeding, overdosing, illness and so on, the numbers of kids that I've known who have not hit the twenty –one year mark is mind numbing. There are times when an old yearbook picture or a name is brought up in conversation and it's hard not to not think of where life would have brought them had they not passed away. But I would venture to say that few of us really ever thought about not making it past high school. Life, years and the road ahead would seem a given. The thing is none of us know how many years we've been granted and even if we live to ninety- nine, it's still a pretty quick act one to five in the scheme of time.

Not too long ago I was on my way to an appointment when I made a quick stop to grab a few things from the grocery store. With only a handful of items I made my way to the express line fumbling for my cash and already thinking about where I had to be next. My mental check list was interrupted with a, "*Hey, Lawler!*" I looked up to see one of my kids who graduated a few years before. She was a bubbly, quirky little thing who was eager to catch me up on how life was going; or at least an abridged version to fit in the time frame of grocery check in and check out. Her eyes sparkled and the smile on her face was radiant with joy. It was nice to see her again. I wasn't short with her, just in a hurry. But it was nice to see her, to hear that life was going pretty well and then it was on to my appointment. That was a Saturday afternoon. She was killed in a car accident a few days later. I kept thinking, why didn't I take the time to listen, ask a few more questions and be a little more attentive?

I can't hit the rewind button, but my heart is sad for another life snuffed out. She didn't wake that morning having any idea it would be her last. Fragile. Life is so very fragile.

One of my greatest fears in life is to squander away the time I've been given only to reach a point where I'm immersed in complacency. To live void of challenge, passion and vision is something that causes me to take pause and contemplate the road in which I travel. So often change or the shifts in life's altering tides can evoke emotions such as fear, trepidation and anxiety. But a life that has no change in horizon or latitude leads to a static nowhere. A dead end road is a desolate and lonely place to end up. Heavy concept, but after being hit with some heavy bricks in life reinforcing the realization that life is fleeting, it's just easier to cut to the chase.

The dates on the calendar never flip back; they always move forward. You can choose to avoid removing each new numeric day that arrives, but the reality is that it will change whether you like it or not. Refuse to become stuck in the pause button state of life always looking back and never allowing yourself to settle into the present. The days go by too quickly for that.

Have you ever noticed a pond where there is no outsourcing or incoming flow of water? With time that small body of water accumulates a large reserve of bacteria and algae. It attracts mosquitoes and all kinds of precarious creatures. The funny thing is that what was once a visibly still and relatively pure body of water becomes slowly overtaken by scum and algae blanketing the surface. Very often an odor will be emitted. The stench is intense and the appearance of the pond isn't a pretty sight. Stay with me here. When we as humans settle, thus allowing ourselves to just sort of go through the motions of life, there is risk of transitioning from pond to 'bog.'

Complacency and remaining fixated on solely you and you alone paves the way for an existence of just being. Am I saying they're emitting an odor and accumulating human forms of algae? Not always, but there are those who allow complacency to morph into cynicism and, as I coin it, 'me-ism.' So the algae and stench of self-absorption may in fact become the full blown transition to an individual bearing the life form of a 'human bog.' It's a pretty lonely state to be in.

Avoiding a state of '*me-ism*' takes intentional effort simply because it's exactly what our society preaches and embraces. To me or not to me is the impending struggle we all will inevitably be faced with. Our value by society's standards is typically weighed by the degrees you possess, the car you drive, the house you live in and the clothes you wear. It's quantity not quality. There is nothing wrong with having material items and enjoying the fruits of your labor. The balance is found in keeping it in check where the extras in life aren't what define you or keep you from the things that really matter. There is so much stuff out there to distract us it is mind- boggling. We want our kids to be grounded and not totally self-absorbed, but every turn they take they're up against the newest iphone, how many likes they received on an Instagram post to validate their popularity, the latest shoes in style, what type of car they are driving and a million other things they believe define them as an individual, but in reality they are investing in materials that slip through the colander of substance. It's the polar opposite of what defines character.

We're indoctrinated with messages of beauty, youth and materials that are all fleeting and one-dimensional. After hours, months and years of these false messages how can we then expect our kids to know the difference between that which is artificial and substance? They are watching by the examples we are setting and it is only through the messages and words spoken by the adults that they come in contact with that maintaining a healthy perspective is attainable.

There's a reflection in the mirror
with eyes of blue
and hair that has been gently kissed by the sun
she's looking closely examining
any defects in the curves of her hips
or the small of her back
And she winces
The Coach handbag with ripped jeans
and form- fitting top
can't conceal her sadness
It cannot hide the fact that
there is a mask that cracks
A heart that aches and so desperately
wants to be that girl
on the cover of the magazine
The one that she see follows on Instagram
Or the one on her favorite show Thursday night
Why can't she be that?
Why are there imperfections?
Why can the mirror not reflect a different image?
Other than the one her eyes believe is so unacceptable
and deplorable?
Why did the jeans, bag, shoes and shirt not do the trick?
Wasn't it supposed to? Why is she still sad?
Why does she still question her beauty?
Why is there a sense of hollowness and nothingness?
Why?

At the end of the day the jeans, fine wine and fancy cars are not the answer and cannot provide fulfillment. You're probably thinking, *'it sure makes things easier.'* But does it? If you look at the countless celebrities with all their stuff, at the end of the day their divorce rates and level of addiction is far greater than the general public. After trying to fill themselves with objects there is a point that even that becomes old, routine and meaningless. The search continues to find something, but there is little to no substance in 'stuff.' Our youth seek to emulate a group of people who are no different than themselves other than the fact that they have more money than they know what to do with. Other than that, there is nothing separating them from us.

All of these materials in life will seem less important the firmer grasp we have on what really matters. When we fill-up on stuff it's pretty similar to trying to water your plants with a watering can that has a bunch of holes on the bottom. It might look like you can get the job done, but it just can't be done. A whole lot of effort is invested into something that will always fall short. The truth is when we step outside of ourselves the filling up comes a bit easier. Truth, substance and selflessness have the ability to knock your socks off if you let it. It's as simple as holding the door for an elderly person, volunteering at a soup kitchen, making eye contact and giving a simple hello to a stranger on the street or clearing out clothes not really used in your closet and dropping them off to your local Goodwill store. You don't have to go full fledge Mother Theresa; the fact is that the "pay it forward" mentality is a process that will overtime become contagious.

There is just something awesome about having an opportunity to reach beyond the surface and gain a sense of making a difference. You just begin to feel good about doing good.

One of the most humbling experiences in my life was during a stint in Belarus the summer before my junior year of college. I was nineteen, pretty naïve and entered a world that I knew next to nothing about. It was an opportunity to work with other college students who attended the University of Belarus in Minsk, the city's capital. We played soccer, shared our faith, chatted about politics, both of our country's histories, shared coffee and essentially had a cultural exchange with other college students.

I made a quick connection with a girl who was the same age as me attending University. Anya was petite, with long dirty brown hair and a square like face. She was one of the kindest people I had ever met. I remember the first time we met up at a local park and were sitting on a bench chatting about our lives and both pretty eager to learn from one another. When you're nineteen you have a tendency to still cling to the blind concept that you possess a good deal of worldly knowledge. I have to say the moment I landed in Belarus that all pretty much disintegrated.

There was something about walking in a world that I didn't even know existed on the map a little over a year ago. This land and her people had been subjected to such heartache, financial hardships and oppression that I had only heard about during history lessons. Her reality challenged my perception of everything I had ever known. So many of her family members had passed away from past wars, starvation or illness. My heart ached and my head just seemed to spin. How could I have been so unaware of a world only a nine- hour plane ride away?

Anya shared how very proud her family was that she would be the first in her family to graduate from University. She was proud of her accomplishments, but there was something that seemed to linger that she wasn't telling me. She lived with her mother and two siblings. Her father had grown sick a number of years ago and passed on. There was something hollow and broken in the description of her father's death. I couldn't figure out what it was. With tears in her eyes she cut the tension asking about my family, university and so on. I found my description and story abridged due to how embarrassed I was at the cushy type of life I had compared to hers. But my emotional attachment and depth of empathy for the Bella Russians would only grow with my friendship with Anya.

The next week Anya invited me over to her flat for lunch. I hopped the tram from our hotel and rang the bell outside her flat as she greeted me with a great big hug. Her sparkling green eyes resonated with joy that I had followed through with my promise to meet. As she held the door and led me through the darkened corridor I had never been in a place like this. I felt like I was in a dilapidated abandoned warehouse that the people here called home. We walked up two flights of steps and after a few moments she had her keys out and jingling making our way into her home.

It couldn't have been more than 400 feet in dimensions with the kitchen, living room and bedrooms seeming to all interconnect into one space. The lighting was dim, but the light in the eyes of Anya, her mother and two younger brothers could have powered the city for a year. Her mother held my cheeks and sputtered a few words in Russian and I nodded. *"She says, welcome to our home. We are so very honored to have you come and have lunch with us."* Anya's mother took my hand and led me to a table that rose two or three feet off the ground. I joined them, Indian style, engrossed in conversation and very anxious to spend the afternoon with such dynamic people.

As plates were laid out on the table and dishes were placed in a decorative fashion brimming with a substantial amount of food a knot swelled in my throat and I desperately fought off tears from swelling in my eyes. I recalled during a briefing back home how the average income in Belarus was approximately thirty US dollars a month. Before me was equivalent to this family's food for the week. This was laid out for me as their guest. I wanted to scream, *Take it back! put it in the fridge for your next few meals. This is yours. This is food for your family that you need!* But every last detail and scrap of food was being presented to me.

My stomach was in knots recalling how many times over the years I ordered too much at a restaurant only to toss it in the trash. Or all the times I discarded leftovers in my fridge just because I simply didn't feel like eating it. Such great waste. Such excess in my world and here I sat with feeling utterly ashamed.

There was food that I couldn't identify. A dish or two that had a scent that one might turn their nose to. But at that moment I was honored to be with these people. They gazed at me awaiting my response, my approval. Sitting there all I wanted to do was throw my arms around them and weep, hug and love on these people who had bestowed more to me than anyone I had ever met. This gift, this gesture was from the heart.

I'm not even sure what our conversation was or the color of the rug we sat on or the music playing in the background. What I will never forget were the smiles, the selflessness and the unimaginable love expressed that shattered my view of what life is really about. Anya and I kept in touch over the next few years. We wrote letters back and forth. Her mother passed a short time after my return to the States.

Anya graduated from University. We both graduated the same year. But that would be the last time I heard from her. I knew she was sick. She had shared with me years prior that when she was in the womb her mother, and countless others, were affected by the radiation from Chernobyl: a nuclear explosion that occurred in the Ukraine, but winds had carried all the soot and devastating residue pretty much dumping it on Minsks's doorstep. There were so many who had contracted strange ailments, diseases and cancers that would have implications for generations. It's a catastrophe that will linger long beyond my lifetime and the pathetic thing is that I had never even taken the time to learn of Chernobyl or Belarus before my stint here.

I had lost a dear friend. Now, years have passed and there are times I think of her, her mother and that afternoon sipping coffee and sharing a meal that will be carried with me eternally. Belarus turned my world upside down and I am forever grateful for that. Life is short, but precious. Anya inspired me to live and encourage others to live fully with receptive ears, a sensitive heart and open arms. She taught me that regardless of age, we can make a difference.

Allow yourself the opportunity to go beyond your comfort zone. You don't have to go to Belarus for this to happen. It's simply allowing your eyes to see and observe in a manner that you haven't before. There is so much hurt, sadness and heaviness in the hearts of so many today. It takes buying the officer in line a cup of coffee, giving a hug to the friend going through a separation, washing a car of a neighbor who might be faced with an illness or passing out a few bagged lunches when you're in the city to those without homes. Eyes and hearts can be opened if we allow them and I promise you if you take that step you will never, ever be the same.

Linear Equations

A while ago I sat in my office chatting with a student about their frustration with decisions friends were making and how overwhelming it was to see the ones they cared so greatly for self -destructing. They sat and listened questioning if the words they shared were indeed making any difference.

I grabbed a marker and paper off of my desk and proceeded to draw a line horizontally from one side of the paper to the other. I then placed a distinct mark on the line about a quarter of the way from the beginning of the line. *"This is where you are now in your life,"* I said and proceeded to have my finger follow the line along the paper; *"and this is your life in ten years. You may never know the significance of your decisions, the extension of yourself towards others and the dedication you have to truly be a friend to those around you for many years. And in some cases you may never know."* The student's eyes were filled with tears and I continued, *"but I promise you that the impact you will have on their hearts and lives will be immeasurable way beyond this year's biggest keg party, who's dating the quarterback or who was homecoming queen. All of that gets lost and becomes a distant memory that no one cares about once you walk off of that field for graduation. But I promise you that your efforts, your caring will be remembered and have an impact beyond your wildest imagination."*

We can become so disheartened in the moment. It's keeping in mind that our lives are one long linear line that we cannot grasp either what each stage will hold or the impact made along the way. One stone that skips along the surface of a pond may look insignificant, but we have no way of knowing how or when that small pebble will play a much bigger role in the scheme of things. Pretty epic if you allow your mind to wrap around the big picture.

On the flip side of things, that line running along that paper has a beginning and an end. Every human is gifted with one life. It's essentially a fleeting moment in time; a vapor that appears briefly then fades. In the scheme of things, regardless of how long our lives span it's a quick blip on the screen of time. We're here and then we're gone. It's like that ten to one countdown that flashes before the start of a movie.

What I find mind boggling is how few actually pause and reflect on our mortality and the fact that the curtain is going to close at one time or another. Most human beings have the tendency to avoid thinking about death and life's inevitable end at all costs. The topic itself often evokes a sense of fear or panic. Personally, this reality has brought forth a constant sense of keeping priorities and vision in check. Taking the time to pause and consider that this isn't forever brings forth the whisper of our own mortality. Instead of avoiding the obvious and closing our eyes hoping it will just go away, stare it in the face. If you do, I promise that it will alter your outlook on how you live your life and treat those you come in contact with.

I stand upon this rock with crashing waves below
and infinite skyline before me
My arms stretched open wide and chest pushed out
toward wind and elements
It is all before me, yet all behind me
Each glimmer and every speck
of grandeur absorbed
Life is past, present and future
and still so much more
I will take it in stride
I will embrace, grasp and hold on strong
But may I refrain from shunning this greatness
That at times may seem too much, overwhelming
This gift, I pray, will not be squandered
Come rain, wind or cold I shall stand
and weather this storm
Calmness will come, although I know not when.
I will continue with faith and hope not to waiver
Open arms, open heart and willing spirit.

For some reason in our society avoiding the topic of our mortality is accepted and in most instances expected. Strange reality, since all of us are in the same boat. My statements aren't intended to be morbid, but a truth that if taken into consideration has the potential to alter not only how life is perceived, but the manner in which it is lived.

A number of years ago while sitting on the beach in the early morning hours watching the sun peak through the horizon this truth hit me. I may live into my late nineties with children, grandchildren and even great grandchildren; or my last breath could be within a few hours or possibly days. It wasn't anything that freaked me out, but it's hard to not think that you'll be around forever. There will be many sunrises and sunsets long after I leave this place.

Millions of footprints left upon the shoreline that will all be eventually erased by another incoming tide. Realistically speaking, none of us have the knowledge or foresight to know the exact hour or day of our demise. But what if we did know the exact time and place of our death? If there was the choice to take a quick peak at our own final chapter in life, would you? If so, would it evoke more fear than determination in how we lived out our every day?

If you were to pause and think about what if there were only five years, two years or even three months remaining on the clock of life; would it alter the manner in which you lived? If today were to be your final sunset could you say with confidence that the years were full, appreciated and lived in a way that doesn't make you shake your head with regret? My intention is to grease up the wheels in your head and hope as we proceed the wheels will begin to spin. Some will be quicker or slower than others.

Is life merely a routine? Is each day a blur that morphs into months, years and ultimately decades? Has it become color that has faded into a murky hue of gray? It's easy to assume the time line before us will press on into our later years. But what if it all came to an abrupt end today? What if you were shifted from present to past tense and with that had the opportunity to sit and watch your life on the big screen?

What would the DVD version of your life look like? Would it be a best seller teeming with action, depth and substance? Or would it receive a two star rating that most wouldn't bother to take off the shelf? Has my own life and the road traveled impacted others? Has yours? Or have the distractions and shallow materials of society wrapped themselves into a tight ball of string that seems to have no real beginning or end?

If we all had our own DVD version of our lives, what would the subtitles read and how enticing would a review be? Would your version go straight to the discount rack or be a potential blockbuster? The vast majority reading this will be more inclined to walk the aisles of Target and Old Navy than Sax Fifth Avenue or Versace. We're not leaving flames of celebrity behind. And for me, that's just fine and a life absent from the shallowness of Hollywood and Entertainment Tonight can unquestionably consist of substance and be deemed a four star rating. The more insight I gain about life and the time spent with aching hearted teens the more absurd and insignificant celebrity magazines, Hollywood-esque TV shows seem. The crazy just isn't alluring.

A number of years ago before taking a six month hiatus throughout the Pacific I spent some time in California. I was prepping to take a short -term gig on the North island of New Zealand, but wanted to take an adequate amount of time trekking through portions of California. Most of my travels were determined by surf conditions, opportunities to explore hidden gems off the beaten path along with open couch availabilities. So staying in L.A. for longer than twenty-one hours wasn't on the agenda, it just sort of happened in transit to San Diego.

I was gearing up for a few months of nature, serenity and the rugged outdoors. Los Angeles was the last place I wanted to be. Smog, traffic and chaos made my heart rate pick up pace. But I was there and you make the best of your circumstances. A few hours after touching down at LAX airport I went for a walk along Hollywood Boulevard. It was the same strip that I had always seen flashed on the screen of award shows, sitcoms and music videos. I guess it is what some would consider the nucleus of Hollywood with the Chinese Theater and stars names embossed upon the walkways.

There seemed to be countless names of famed actors and actresses, singers and comedians that seemed to go on forever. Many fellow tourists clicked pictures or paused to reflect on the name etched on the earth below them. It was something of a mad house really watching people from all over the world discussing, posing and lingering around names that, for some, had been deceased for many years. It was a little weird to observe.

In their lifetime Frank Sinatra, Bing Crosby, Lucille Ball and many others were idolized and adorned by fans. They possessed profound talent, fame and fortune. I didn't know any of those individuals personally and my intention is not to judge them. But as I walked those streets and watched the thousands of feet stepping over or on those embossed names it made the wheels of my mind spin. Whether alive or dead these individuals achieved fame, fortune and what so many seek after. But, in the end, they're just another name. Every day thousands of feet walk on their names that line Hollywood streets, cigarette butts are flicked unintentionally their way and some take a glance at a name that they can't recognize.

Life goes on, the world does not stop. People cry, light candles, place flowers at doorsteps and grieve. But the grief and mourning for those they touched comes to an end at one point or another. The stock market opens the next day, people still run into Starbucks for their latte and go home to their families at night. The globe keeps on spinning and the stars continued to be aligned. In the end, fame and status doesn't get you a pass from expiring. I guess that sounds harsh. But are our efforts as individuals focused enough on others, giving back, investing in what comes after us? Or does the focus continue to be more intrinsically focused perpetuating further self-ism and hollowness?

The choice, whether famous or an unknown, is for us to make. An individual who carried the torch of fame and character with true dignity was Paul Newman. I remember the first time I saw Cool Hand Luke. Paul Newman made an impression on me as a sixteen year old. But what left a greater, lasting impression will be the countless lives he has changed through his charities over the years. The face of Mr. Newman has adorned salad dressing, marinara sauce and vegetables. Supermarket aisles across the nation carry a label with a face that will carry on in the hearts of millions. There will even be those who know him more as the man on the label than the actor. He used fame to benefit others and he had a vision that connected with people's hearts, not their egos. Mr. Newman, will long be remembered for his substance. The cars, homes and glitz will fade, but his mission will press on for generations.

I would dare to say a headstone has never read, worked forty years straight sixty hours a week, never took a sick day, had an impressive five bedroom home with a pool and a Mercedes. None of that matters when the curtains have closed and act five of life has drawn to an end. There is no peanut gallery standing to their feet in a round of applause because of your financial portfolio or at the number of high-end handbags you had lined in your bedroom closet.

That is one thing I'm pretty confident of. No golf clap goes to the man who snagged the biggest house overlooking the Pacific or woman accumulating the most impressive stock portfolio. In the ebb and tide of life there is none who can bring stocks, 401(k) plans, or summer homes with them. It is worthless and is like fine sand slipping through fingertips. Here one-second, but gone the next. Is there anything wrong with job security, a financial cushion and a comfortable lifestyle? No. But it can be an awful challenge attempting to not enter the 'rat-race' scurrying always towards a bigger house, nicer car with endless wants for material objects that you just have to have.

A few times a year I pay a visit to Odd Fellow Cemetery right off of Main Street in the town I grew up in. There's something within me, in a non-morbid sense, that feels a connection here and maybe even a sense of solace. I have many old friends and people I've loved over the years laid to rest on this small plot of land.

Maybe that explains a little. It 's a visit that is humbling, but also my reminder of why I live my life in the manner I do personally and professionally. I'm an addictions counselor and on top of that I'm a wife, parent, daughter, sister, aunt, friend and neighbor. As I walk in silence among the countless headstones it isn't morbidity that draws me here, but the faces, voices and memories that were once here and now are just faded memories that cause an acute pain in my heart.

So many lives cut short. So many I sat next to in class, rode the school bus with everyday for years, shared secret and some I truly loved. Young faces that will remain forever in a freeze frame of youth and vitality. Each face here has become a freeze frame photo that will never step forward into the next natural stage of life. That's a heavy reality.

Each of these wonderful young people left, in their own way, an imprint on my heart. I often think of where they would be now and if the life I am living and have lived would make many of them proud. It may sound strange, but part of me feels there is an obligation to strive harder, live fuller and more acutely in place of each of these faces.

As I walk into the doors of my high school each day I contend with the voices in my head, the perpetual fear of losing another. There is so much out there to fear, but the reality is that so much is out of our hands. The truth is that not one of us knows for certain how long we have and I use my strolls through Odd Fellow to remind me that I am indeed mortal, each day is a gift and I dare not take it for granted. What shall I do this day to make a difference? How will I live in a manner that what is left behind is long lasting?

As a young person I associated cemeteries with death, the illusive end and a stark coldness that made me walk a bit quicker if passing by and find a distraction to shift my attention. Over time how we perceive things is all about how we choose to view what lies in front of us. The cemetery didn't change, my perception did. It no longer causes a shiver through my spine, but has instead become another source for learning and refraining from getting pulled into the vacuum of complacency and 'me-ism' that is prominently displayed in any direction you look. Every aspect of our lives is all about how we choose to view and perceive it. And we have the ability to alter our perceptions of things if we so choose.

The interesting thing about our mortality is that, in the end, we will all return to dust. There is a date listed for birth and one that documents date of demise. The only thing separating the two dates is a dash. The dash holds it all. The dash holds everything from first breath to last.

Recycle the Superficial

I'm a sucker for gingerbread houses. They're just all around Christmas goodness. If I could build a life size one, it would be tempting to rock out the frosted windows, gum drop roof lined roof and candy cane street lamps. Some ginger bread houses are elaborately decorated and stunning while others are pretty basic. But trying to really live in one is pretty unrealistic. Why? Because the materials the home are constructed of are delicate and the foundation is inadequate. Where am I going with this?

If we attempt to establish our identities and direction in life with a weak and wavering foundation, we're in for trouble. A house built on sand will inevitably be swatted around by the wind and weakened by the sea. In order to withhold the tempests that we face as human beings, there must be rooting and there must be substance. When these are instilled at a young age, it paves the road for young people and adults to withhold the storms of life and possess a healthier perspective of what does and does not matter.

Young and old are inundated with faulty messages. Every day we are bombarded with air brushed images that define what beauty is supposed to look like, told to believe sex is not sacred and is rather casual and uninhibited, TV glorifying those who scheme, lie, cheat and accrue the most 'stuff' in their lives. All of us are receiving totally skewed messages and it can be challenging to not have this penetrate our hearts.

A legitimate fear is when young people mimic the priorities set by Hollywood and society, they run a high risk of falling flat on their faces when tested with trials and tribulations of life that money or popularity are not able to solve. The mixed messages being sent are confusing and it is up to parents, educators and mentors to send a clear, bellowing message of truth that is sound and not diluted. Sometimes the truth can sting or even hurt, but get out the bullhorns, wave those hands and may the message being sent be loud and clear.

My feeling is that if we provide an example of the importance of giving back, younger generations will follow en suit. A few years back I hopped on a bus with about twenty kids and rolled into Love Park located in Philadelphia to participate in our Philly Full Fledge Feed. This project was intended to not just provide a meal and clothing to those without shelter, but to knock the socks off of the kids and adults participating. It was meant to cause everyone present to question and distinguish the difference between wants and needs.

We rolled into Philly just shy of rush hour and hopped off the bus with each kid carrying an arm full of boxes, bags filled with bagged lunches and stacks of clothing. They quickly pulled together organizing all the items and setting up an assembly line. I could tell the kids were a bit overwhelmed as about one hundred plus men and women were lined up eagerly awaiting the distribution. Bagged lunches, shirts, shoes, socks and sweatshirts were organized and ready to be handed out. As one after another slowly sifted through piles of clothing examining each item carefully, they beamed with joy at their new possessions.

I stood off to the side and observed each young person who seemed to absorb the magnitude of what was going on around them. Items that they might have found in the back of their closets or stuffed in a drawer that was now someone else's treasure. I could see their minds spinning and thinking, *there was so much more that I could have brought. I didn't know that there were people who had so little.* It was a life lesson being seared into their brains that was not in a classroom, but on a random side street of Philadelphia. There were a few who were so overwhelmed. I watched as their minds experienced a three hundred and sixty degree mental change up soaking in everything around them. It's not often that we take the opportunity to observe, but that's exactly what they were doing.

A handful of students were fixated on the small cluster of men and women comparing and contrasting their goods and beaming with joy and pride. Heads were spinning. Realities were being realigned. I felt a hand on my shoulder. A tall, lanky girl stood next to me with tears in her eyes. *"Lawler, I could have brought three more bags of clothes and shoes that I don't even use. I didn't know. Why didn't I take the time to just...do something? I'm sorry. I'm so sorry."* I consoled her. I hugged and patted her on the back. *"There is a need. There are always needs. My hope is that you guys will take this with you. Everyone here has a story, including us. No one knows the whys and how's of the people around us. It's not up to us to judge. But there are needs. There are heaps of needs. Take what you have experienced today and begin to look at people around you. Know that you have made a difference today, but do not let it stop here. Let yourself leave an imprint on someone's heart. Not a lot of people have let themselves take that step. Take it and it will change you. Let it rock your world."*

My belief is that the twenty kids that day did have their eyes open and that a little seed was planted in their hearts. Each of us has the ability to make a difference, but we have to initiate and we have to be willing to take the step. Paying it forward is a pretty great way to very simply change the world.

Ideas and Suggestions For Going Beyond 'The You'

When attempting to figure out exactly what and where you want to invest your time and serve others it can be overwhelming in more ways than one. *Where do I go? Who do I call? What type of people will I be interacting with?* All of these are great questions!

Here are a few ideas:

• Take a look at services within your community such as: soup kitchen, shelters, food bank, animal shelters, church/ temple needs, Habitat For Humanity projects, Animal Shelters, the Red Cross and the Ronald McDonald House (these are just a few).

• Contact the facility of interest and feel free to ask age restrictions, hours of operation and what your time commitment would be. It's OK to ask!

• Inquire if it's possible for this to be a family event. There can be age restrictions, but that isn't everywhere. Serving together only strengthens a family!

For those of you who may yearn for something a little less structured and home grown, you're always free to make up your own version of serving and reaching out.

Here are a few things that I've made my own projects in the past:

• While traveling abroad in Colombia a few years ago, I tracked down an area orphanage in town and contacted them prior to my departure. I was able to bring an extra suitcase of goods on my journey for a pretty great cause. (point being, if you're going somewhere as a family or individually it's pretty simple to bring a few extra things to drop off at an area soup kitchen, shelter, etc.)

• I spent some time in Jerusalem and was able to work a few hours in the morning at a soup kitchen during my two- week stay. (what a great way to get to meet new people and gain some powerful lessons when the family is on a road trip or stationed somewhere for more than a few days).

• On Thanksgiving and Christmas Eve, my family and I have packed up a few dozen bagged lunches and we head over to Philly where we hand out food to those without a place to live. Handing someone a meal, looking them straight in the eye passes on a message of love and caring that will blow your mind. We hit visible, well -lit and populated areas and there's never been an issue.

If you live in or near a city or economically struggling area there's not much effort exerted throwing an extra bag lunch in your belongings once a week or gathering a bunch of friends to make some food and head in for a few hours of goodness. Community projects are great for friendships!

If you're up for it, make an outreach bucket list. What are things/projects that interest you for the year? Write them down and brainstorm ways to make a thought into a reality. You can do it!

Ingredients For Growth
(and Some Basic Rules For Life...)

- Every young person should have to work in retail or the food industry at some point in their lives. Wiping off ketchup from someone's plate has a strange way of providing some of life's greatest lessons.

- Not everyone gets a trophy. Get over it. In the real world there aren't little golden trophies for everyone in the office or in line for a sandwich.

- Spend an afternoon or evening serving others at least once a year.

- If you empty the ice tray, fill it back up. Common law of life and courtesy.

- When you use the bathroom, flush the toilet and do a follow-up look just to make sure all that should be gone really is.

- Hold the door for the person behind you. They know after semi-eye contact that you know that they are there. It's a courtesy that goes a long way.

- If you smoke, that cigarette you flick out the window of a moving vehicle does not magically get sucked into an abyss of reds and slims somewhere in the great graveyard in the sky. It's trash. It's on the ground and someone has to pick it up. It's gross.

- When in a public place, avoid talking on your cell phone. No one cares about your drama, what you're having for dinner or when soccer practice is. It's rude and inconsiderate.

- Speaking of cell phones....while conversing, put the phone down and make eye contact with the other person. When looking down you and multi-conversing it's annoying and you're going to ask me to repeat what was just said one point two minutes ago.

- Don't talk with your mouth full.

- Buy a person in uniform a cup of coffee at least once a year. What a simple way to say thank you.

- Leave anywhere you visit as you found it. Whether that's the beach, the park or your table at a restaurant. It's no one's job to clean up after you and there's no magical nature fairy that swoops up your rubbish.

- Send a loved one an actual hand written note or card

- Let someone you haven't told in awhile that you love or appreciate them.

Self-Harm

Being a teenager is tough stuff. They are faced with a myriad of challenges that can sometimes feel overwhelming. Our kids have choices as to how they handle stress, sadness, guilt, fear, etc. Expressing their emotions or confiding in another human being may seem like it isn't an option and that's a scary place to be.

In the past decade there has been an increase in self- harm among adolescence. Self-harm is when an individual cuts, punctures or burns himself in sometimes visible and other times not so visible parts of their body. Objects used to inflict pain may include razor blade, scissors, a lit cigarette, a knife, flame from a candle, etc. The list, unfortunately, is kind of endless. When an individual is feeling the pull to harm it may be the closest and most accessible object to them or it can be a very organized, premeditated process. It depends upon the individual.

The reality is that it's a struggle that can't easily be met with "just stop." Self -harm is a form of coping, relieving pain and even expression. When emotions are connected to physical infliction of pain the healing process is one requiring family support that should be accompanied by counseling.

Many of you might be asking what does it look like? There are a few things to keep an eye on. Such as, wearing long sleeve clothing at inopportune times, such as when it's hot out. Hiding marks with bracelets around their wrist. Marks can be masked in more discreet areas such as the inner thigh or on the stomach region. There are many teens who will struggle with this during the course of their adolescence, but many more will know someone who is harming himself/herself in this way.

I've spoken with parents over the years whose children have struggled with self-harm. As a parent it is heart breaking. You desperately want to fix their hurting, but the pain is complex and the solution isn't immediate. Support and counseling can help begin the healing process. One response that can seriously backfire is saying they should just stop doing it or that it's merely silly teenager stuff. When those words spill out of a parent or guardian's lips it is interpreted as anything but helpful. The road to it stopping begins with counseling, support, treatment and time.

The reality is, many of our kids may encounter a friend, classmate or teammate who displays visible cuts on their arms or burns or cuts on their thighs or stomachs. It's uncomfortable to see and sometimes they stay quiet or make an attempt to fix their friend within their peer group. When it comes to self- harm the issues are deeply rooted and professional help can truly do wonders.

My urging is for you to chat with your kids, reassuring them that even with all of their best intentions they cannot have the unrealistic responsibility of keeping something like this amongst friends or trying to fix it themselves. Some students may believe that any adult interaction will make things worse. Talking to a parent, older sibling or guidance counselor can get things started in the right direction. There really are many great counselors and programs out there.

Although the process may seem daunting, your insurance carrier can give you a list of in-network counselors and or programs in your area. There is no harm in contacting your student's guidance office, mental health service on a college campus or even friends who may recommend someone they feel like they or a loved one has connected with. There is power in networking!

Thoughts from a graduate:

"I didn't really like to relate to others. I felt that I wanted to be different and I wanted my pain to be the only thing that set me apart from others. I was very twisted in my teen years after the loss of my older sister. I sought pain before anything else and I wanted to feel that pain by myself. In my sophomore year of high school when my sister died I was suicidal and dating a 22 year old. I was so empty inside so I started cutting and self-mutilating. I would do anything to feel anything.

How did I break free? Well, I saw my selfishness. I saw myself for who I really was; a scared little girl that just needed someone to tell her what her place was in this screwed up world. The only solace I ever found was when I was deep in God's word doing life with Him."

Self-harm does not have to define who a teenager is. The struggle is real and a part of them, but it is not who they are. The young lady who shared about her struggles felt trapped, empty and consumed by the pain in her life.

Ultimately, it was her faith that allowed her to break from self-harming. It has been an overwhelming joy watching the growth of this young lady over the years. She is not only a survivor, but an inspiration. It's awesome when the young people you encounter end up teaching you life lessons and providing encouragement through their resilience.

Just Say No...

"Just say no" was an infamously popular phrase coined by Nancy Reagan to combat the war on drugs in the eighties. Although Nancy had the best of intentions, it's a method to a madness that isn't the most effective. Use, experimentation and dependence all interconnect in ways that having a simple 'no' as the solution is ineffective. So without sounding ridiculously cynical, I'll expound.

Our kids are faced with a myriad of choices on a daily basis and the decision whether or not to succumb to pressure can be daunting. A dilemma we are now facing on a national level is the gap that exists in defining what is considered a drug. What falls in that gray area constantly is over the counter medicines, marijuana and prescription pills.

Personal definitions of what is considered off-limits and what is fair game is changing constantly. What is and isn't OK typically doesn't jive with the law, not that this is something that is in the forefront of people's minds. This gray area has created mass confusion and an opportunity for impulsive decisions.

This generation of teens has grown up in a media saturated world. There are plusses and minuses with this. A negative is the access to drug trends, sites showing exactly how to use certain substances and the means in which you can obtain them. This is where monitoring what sites your child visits on social media sites is crucial. You can You Tube pretty much anything from how to prepare for your first LSD trip, the proper technique for dabbing, observing some random person in the cyber world trip on MDMA or tripping on Molly. It's insane. So if you weren't sure about what a drug was, you're not only seeing what it looks like, but what it actually does to you.

There are no parental warnings, FDA advisories or anything saying, *this isn't such a good idea.* Social media places anything and everything at our kid's fingertips. From Meth to Molly it's super frightening. When anyone can watch dozens of videos online of people tripping and not dying, it can become easy to minimize the severity of using certain drugs. That reality is scary. If they didn't die or seem really bad off with their trip, how bad can it really be? Holy of all craziness. We are in an uphill battle and as parents, community members and aunts and uncles we have to have some grasp on what's out there. Spend some time clicking through Google or You Tube and know that ignorance is a very dangerous thing in the world of drugs.

In the drug realm what I find fascinating is how social media has fed into the growth of young people experimenting. Being in a picture posted at a party passed out surrounded by empty Smirnoff bottles, inhaling from a gravity bong or taking a tablet of acid are just a few of the posts I've scrolled through over the years. So many of our kids equate being cool with the likes they get from a picture and that strange form of peer pressure means posting things they might not typically be comfortable with just in the name of letting their friends see them in the moment. An issue then connects with fifteen year olds posting things that can kick them in the butt come time to apply to college or for the twenty three year old submitting applications for a job. Once a picture is posted that you are tagged in, it never really goes away. It can be found.

If you were to conduct a survey of teens and adults in your community, the vast majority would attest to a friend or relative who uses some form of prescription medication. Medicine can do wonderful things when used for its intended purpose, but with its presence comes great responsibility. This is where the gap is seemingly massive between knowledge in the area of what meds have highest risk for addiction, what they do and their long-term implications. The gray area is our mortal enemy. It's causing medical professionals to overprescribe, have the propensity to have itchy fingers to pen a prescription without pressing the patient enough about their personal history with addiction as well as their family history of addiction. The general public does not have the insight or background on these particular drug's potential for addiction. They are misinformed and overmedicated. Meds can help, without question, but you have to be *informed, informed, informed.*

What I have found disturbing is the knowledge and perception towards prescription medications. If meds are not prescribed to you then you aren't supposed to ingest them. But after thousands of commercials with the little cloud following animated characters that are suddenly transformed by a pill, the message that young and old are receiving is that when I'm sad, need a pick me up or simply want to feel differently, a quick fix is found in that little pill. Whether it be Adderall, Xanax or any type of Percocet or muscle relaxer, most are aware that pills will change how they feel without realizing what it can do to their systems as well as the addictive component. In reality, we all possess some fraction of invincibility in our mind.

Nationwide we have a pill-popping epidemic that runs the spectrum of sixteen year olds to sixty year olds. Pills seem less dirty than the higher tiered drugs like cocaine and meth. They're easy to obtain and the potency to get you up or down is part of their enticement. It's frightening how there is no face to depict a user or an addict. Every type of kid, when fed enough lies and twisting of truths about how wonderful a pill is can be seduced into using. It's critical to be pro-active and knowledgeable (to some extent) of what the pill is as well as the physical effects in can have on both a short and long term basis. Knowledge is power.

Key aspects to pill abuse:

• Prescription pills are typically accessed from a relative or friend's medicine cabinet.

• If not directly from a medicine cabinet, then it has a great likelihood that it was obtained from a friend/ relative who stole it from someone they know.

• Pills, hands down, are the new bridge between recreational drug use and the transition to harder drugs such as cocaine and heroin, but there are those who keep their drug of choice limited pills.

• Teens and adults are often self-diagnosing themselves as anxious, depressed, in pain, etc. then personally justifying self-medicating with pills.

• Nationally, we are in a frightening place with heroin and the vast majority of users started with OxyContin knowing that it's a pain pill, but unaware of its potency and rapid prospect for addiction.

This is a nationwide epidemic that is not going away anytime soon. I urge you to have a chat with your child, family members and close friends about their perception of pills. This paves the way for what they do or do not know as well as allotting for an opportunity to discuss what to do if they know of someone who is using. The truth is that medication can do wonderful things when it is used properly in a manner that has been prescribed by a physician. Take the time to peruse your own medicine cabinet, see what's in there and do what's needed to make sure that whatever is in there isn't easily accessible.

Common reasons why people experiment:

• Studying, trying to keep attentive, lose weight: Adderall or Ritalin (stimulants that have the opposite effect on someone without A.D.D or A.D.H.D)

• Unwind, space out: Xanax or Valium

• Euphoria, totally sedated: Oxycontin

I have to come clean and say anytime I hear "Oxycontin" or "Oxycodone", my stomach tightens. Out of all the prescription pills that I have encountered these suckers are dangerously deceiving. It's an innocent pill that has swooped in, shaken and unhinged so many, young and old. It leaves them broken and often in the clutches of an opiate that overtakes the body and mind.

What I have witnessed is the progression to heroin begins with Oxycontin. Oxy, a pain pill, is very commonly prescribed to subdue extreme pain or discomfort. What doctors generally do not disclose is that oxy's potency and addictive prospects. The fact is that those prescribed this med can very easily become addicted. At the same time, young people very often do not perceive pills as falling under the umbrella of drugs. That white pill is perceived as harmless, a nice high and very quickly that pill triggers higher level of use and sometimes is the bridge to heroin.

So, what is **Heroin**? What does a user look like? Our preconceived notions are very often incorrect. Heroin is a drug that once you step across that line, it is a life long battle that is gutting.

WHAT is Heroin:

• Derived from morphine – it's an opiate and is classified as a depressant.

• Impacts the brain and the body's perception of pain.

• Usually comes in powder form (white to dark brown).

HOW is it used?

• Most common way = injected into the vein

• Snorted via powder form

• Laced in marijuana (this can be super scary if the user is unaware).

• Smoked

- **Paraphernalia**: includes small baggies or vials, needles, spoons and water bottle caps (used to cook it)

EFFECTS of use:

• SUPER addictive. The user can become hooked after their first use

• High lasts for a couple of hours feeling a surge of euphoria and a sort of 'gumby like' feeling through their body

• After the high wears off = drowsy, slowing of motor skills, constricted pupils and vomiting

<u>Signs of USE:</u>

• Pin- point pupils

• Sweating – excessive, regardless of the weather

• Inconsistent sleeping patterns

• Weight loss ++

• Nodding off

• Noticeable apathy

<u>LONG TERM effects of use:</u>

• Drugs impact everyone differently. Some noticeable implications of use can range from first use to a few months of use. Everyone, as with any drug, is effected differently.

• Some standard effects: collapsed veins, infection of their heart lining, respiratory issues

• Tolerance increases = need for higher doses as use progresses

• With an increase of frequency or the amount = physical dependence

<u>WITHDRAWAL:</u>

• When the high wears off the desire to use escalates and this can be physically and psychologically lethal

- Physical implications: muscle pain, insomnia, diarrhea, vomiting, cold flashes and jerking of body parts or twitching

- Sudden withdrawal CAN be lethal.

A few summers ago I backpacked throughout Columbia, but started my trek in Bogota. I found a great little hostel with a breathtaking backdrop of mountains and fields of coffee plants. The first night in Bogota I ended up chatting with a really nice local guy who was hanging in the hostel, the owner was a friend of his, and he proceeded to share that he lost everything, including his daughter, when he lived in France and felt defeated by heroin.

He chatted and I listened until about five in the morning. Let's just say after that very long session I had an open tab at the restaurant he cooked at for the remainder of my stay. It was a perk in my book. He was a really nice guy devastated by his addiction and even a few years into recovery, he realized how every day was a new beginning and one day further in prevailing, but it was something he was still petrified of. I guess my counsel was appreciated so it was passed onto another guest at the hostel whom I had learned was watching over her boyfriend as he was trying to detox from heroin in a dorm room. She sought me out for advice and guidance. The first words out of my mouth were, *"I'm not a medical professional. I'm just a high school counselor."* That meant nothing. She heard of my words the night prior and now the counseling domino effect was in full swing.

My heart was heavy and anxiety seemed to overtake my body. It was insane. He was locked alone trying to ride it out and the occasional times he popped out for something to eat, for a smoke or fresh air I wasn't around to lay eyes on him. But the times outside his door there were screams, shouting pounding of fists against the walls and door. It was like a caged animal was desperate to break free. Breaking free of either a physical or psychological addiction can be the biggest challenge of your life and I am so very grateful it's one I have never had to contend with. I can't tell you that the outcome with this guy was good or bad. The guy needed medical attention and it wasn't something anyone I spoke to was willing to seek out. So being that he and his friends were unwilling to compromise in seeking medical attention I moved on. I couldn't force him to get help.

I caught a plane two days later to Santa Marta where jungles and surf were on my agenda. A lesson that I've become all too familiar with over the years has been that you can never force anyone to receive treatment and expect a positive outcome. The choice, even if it's reluctant, has to be their own otherwise counsel and guidance are given in vain.

Loved ones and friends cannot work harder than the one that they are fighting for. It just doesn't add up. That's a tough reality to digest. None of us really think that addiction can swoop in and claim someone we love, but it's something that has a grasp on more lives we can wrap our heads around. But the stepping stone usually begins with gate ways such as prescription pills. There is no longer a 'type' of person who uses and that's a frightening reality. I believe the more we talk about it, chat with our kids and loved ones and guard ourselves in knowing how to deter access then we have more working for us than against us.

Medical professionals can do wonderful things, but you MUST be your own advocate. It's OK to ask questions. There's nothing wrong in researching and inquiring about what the prescription tablet might be recommending. Be informed and aware of the plusses, negatives and in-betweens of different medications. There is a window of time for medications to be absorbed by your blood stream, but be keenly aware of any drastic changes and inform your doctor if you feel significant changes. Ask questions, advocate for yourself and be in tune with your body.

A number of years ago I had a student in my office shaking, scared and seeking out my help because of prescription pills. He didn't do anything wrong. He had his wisdom teeth taken out. His dentist wrote a scrip with the designated amount to take. He did exactly that, as per instructed. The second day in he started to shake, popped an extra pill and started thinking about them. He didn't want to. Both physically and psychologically there was a desire to take more. We were now only in day three. He was visibly shaken, taken off guard. This was someone who liked to be in charge of himself, know what he was doing and now all of that was unraveled. We called mom, help was pursued, but he was lucky. How many others are taken off guard? Advocate for you and your family, because if you don't no one else will.

Cocaine is another drug that has been around for a long time and isn't phasing out anytime soon. Whether in powder or rock (crack) form, it's super dangerous.

WHAT is Cocaine:

• Derived from the leaves of a cocoa plant – it's a stimulant

• Impacts the brain and the body's perception of pain

• Usually comes in powder form (most commonly) or in a harder, rock form (crack)

HOW is it used?

• Most common way = snorted

• Snorted via powder form

• Laced in marijuana (this can be super scary if the user is unaware)

-Paraphernalia: includes small clear baggies or vials, some type of flat surface that will have slice marks for chopping white residue (mirror, cd case), item to cut up cocaine (license, credit card), hollow straws or a rolled up dollar bill

* if they are injecting it: needles, some form of a tie they use to secure around their arm, lighter, a small vessel for 'cooking' the drug

EFFECTS of use:

• VERY addictive. The user can become hooked after their first use or their 22nd use…depends upon the individual. It's kind of a crap- shoot.

Signs of USE:

• Elevated mood

• Enlarged pupils

• Increased energy

• Feelings of invincibility / grandiose perception of self

SHORT TERM effects of use can include:

• Paranoia

• Sense of panic

• Anxiety

• Feeling restless

• Increased heart rate/blood pressure/body temperature

LONG TERM effects of use:

• Drugs impact everyone differently. So noticeable implications of use can range from first use to a few months of use. Everyone, as with any drug, is effected differently.

• Some standard effects: respiratory & cardiac issues, stroke, seizures

• Tolerance increases = need for higher doses as use progresses

• With an increase of frequency or the amount = physical dependence

• When the high wears off the desire to use escalates and this can be physically and psychologically lethal

• Physical implications: fatigue, paranoia, increased anxiety, overwhelming depression, restlessness

• Sudden withdrawal CAN be lethal

ADDICTION... How do you even begin to describe it?

I believe it is an illness that can paralyze, demoralize and gut you. If you think those you love and care for are untouchable, you're sorely mistaken. A user, an addict, no longer has a particular look like we used to see on billboards and posters in the 802. It's scary. It's frightening. It's something we can't keep our heads in the sand any longer. Part of it is genetic. Part of it stems from curiosity. It's when prescriptions are written that lead someone with the best of intentions towards a dependency and a thousand other reasons that have an outcome that can all too easily mow victims down without blinking an eye.

I've witnessed young people get into using for a million reasons that range from: curiosity, over committed and attempting to find more hours in the day, numb themselves, taking meds prescribed to them and unwillingly become addicted, rite of passage with drinking/partying that evolves into binge use more frequently, home life is crap, home life isn't crap and a million plus other reasons. There's no rolling out of bed with the intention of becoming an addict. But when we dabble, walk that fine line and play with fire there are some who escape and some who don't. In the process, in rocks a lot of lives to the core, snuffs others out and wreaks havoc on families.

ADDICTION is REAL and CLAIMING lives,

HEARTS and MEMORIES......

We NEED to TALK about IT!

It CANNOT be LOOKED down UPON.

The DOOR must OPEN so LIVES can BE saved.

WE must COME together.

DO not FIGHT alone.

The Socially Accepted Drug

Eyebrows raise and fingers shake when we hear heroin, cocaine or meth. It's in the tier of super scary drugs. When that focus shifts to alcohol the sense of urgency and concern is kicked down a few notches. We live in a society where it is five o'clock somewhere and addressing the dangers of and potential for dependence can easily be shrugged off.

But here's the deal, in every high school across the nation there are young people who are consuming alcohol in a manner that is setting the pathway for a future of addiction. The funny thing is, when it comes to alcohol so often it isn't until very far down the spectrum of dependence that this is addressed.

As parents, the standards have to be set early on. If you expect your kids to make responsible decisions you have to lead by example. That may range from not consuming alcohol or doing so responsibly with the million decisions that accompany this.

Top five ways to give your kids some seriously non-positive messages:

• If you consume alcohol at most functions (family gatherings, sports events, happy hour gatherings, etc.) your children will equate fun and relaxation with alcohol. Meaning, I can't really have fun without it. This may come across as annoying, but the stark truth is when alcohol is and has to be present at all functions (including at home) the message is as clear as day... alcohol is needed in order to have a good time.

• Allowing your kids to have friends over and provide them alcohol under your roof where they are safe = serious ingredients for something very bad happening somewhere down the line. If you think every kid is going to stay and not drive or they will not drink excessively it will present issues at some point.

- What most don't take into consideration is the liability connected to anything that goes wrong: car crash, unwanted touching/sex, fights with injury, etc.) and how much there is to lose on the hosting home's end. It's just not worth it.

• Being buzzed or intoxicated and driving. So here's the deal, have a designated driver, call an Uber or Lyft and get your awesome responsible, role model hat on. In this day and age there's no excuse to take any risk…not just your family, but mine.

• Conveying to your child that drinking is part of their high school experience.

• Being intoxicated and/or incoherent around your young person where you are not in control of your behaviors and words.

As a parent, you have to choose the stance you are going to take with your young person. But be aware, your kids are watching your actions and if you aren't connecting your behaviors with their verbal guidelines your words will hold little weight. At some point every single young person is going to have the choice to drink whether that's at twelve or twenty-one. I believe responsibility is a huge component in any decision we have to make, but all of that kind of goes to the wayside when alcohol comes into the picture.

We are in a society that is all about shoving in and filling up on as much as possible. It's what I call the fast food mentality. You roll into the drive through and for only ninety-nine more pennies you can super-size your meal. Score! I now get 1,243 more calories for less than a dollar and get to eat a portion size fit for three adults. Sweet!

Here's how this breaks down. Very rarely do you have a young person sitting at a social gathering taking in the flavoring of an 89 glass of merlot or a perfectly chilled Corona. It's a binge, take it all in and live in moment mindset. Boom! We now have a recipe for bad things happening. Moderation is thrown out the window and all bets are off when you're dealing with undeveloped brains and impulsive behaviors.

Some of you may be rolling your eyes at me and that's fine. I encourage you to chat with your kids. Where do you stand and where do you want them to stand? What I will also throw out there is that so easily our kids can enter into patterns of decision making that gets out of hand before they realize it. Chat with them about decisions, risks for addiction as well as for what can happen when alcohol is in the picture with their peers.

Here's what frightens me with alcohol....

• In a vast majority of sexual assaults (not all) or rapes alcohol played a factor. The number of young women in high school or college who have been violated is astronomical & unacceptable.

• The quantity increases along with the pressure to drink when larger groups are involved.

• Our kids brains are not fully developed and the trends with high volumes of alcohol then transitioning to mixing of other drugs is frightening. Alcohol combined with pills, synthetic marijuana or cocaine increases as the decision making process is drastically altered.

• If a young person is scared that they will get in trouble if they call home after consuming alcohol the likelihood of driving under the influence or being a passenger of an intoxicated driver increases.

- How easily dependency can develop with every weekend drinking sessions blurring into the occasional weekday and picking up frequency and quantity.

- The rampant prevalence in heavy drinking and multiple sex partners.

- Increase in aggression that can trigger into destroying property, harming others (fights, assaulting or raping someone).

Alcohol kicks people's butts on a daily basis. Am I getting all prohibitionist on you? No. But I am encouraging you to chat with your kids and convey your expectations. I personally enjoy a good glass of red wine with dinner or a cold beer when grilling. I'm not running around asking anyone to poor their libations down the sink. What I merely encourage is responsible, good decision making.

My heart aches for the many young people who have a parent who struggles with addiction. There are the many who come home to a dad passed out unconscious on the couch or the discomfort of going out to dinner hoping mom won't drink too much and have them praying to get home safely as they drive home in their car. The reality is, that mom or dad more than likely began developing their addiction in high school.

Alcohol destroys lives and rips families apart. Every single day so many of our young people go home to the unknown and that stinks. I believe the more we chat about choices, addiction and recovery the better set we are at preventing a lifetime of heartache. As parents, our words are important but our own actions outweigh what comes out of our mouths. You have the ability to encourage, empower and educate your child in a way no one else on earth is capable of. That can be in either an extremely positive or negative way. So get your positive on!

Trends, Cycles and Patterns

I'm frequently asked about drug trends. The truth is in all corners of the globe, different patches of your state or region the substances being abused will vary. Trends are cyclic and depend upon supply, demand and what's the latest vibe going on that can switch as quickly as the direction of the wind. My urging is to hop on Google and spend some time researching what your area papers are trending on with drugs to just simply typing in "trends." Substances will always be a component in our society. It stinks, but it's reality. Each of us, our kids and our kid's kids, will have decisions to make as to whether we dabble or don't. The more we know provides more insight, more power and gives a better shot in knowing the choices we and the ones we love have to make.

A few drug trends to gain insight on:

• MDMA/Ecstasy: whether it be used at a rave or hanging in a garage with friends these evoke feeling of elation heightening senses that revs the internal organs up due to its stimulant qualities. When the high wears off, just like any drug, there's the desire to return to that state of elation. The issue is with prolonged use it can do a number on your serotonin levels making depression and anxiety become a factor that's hard to shake off.

• Synthetic Marijuana (Spice, K2): made to look like marijuana or even potpourri, but the herbs are chopped up and sprayed with synthetic materials that are supposed to mimic thc. The issue is, this stuff can have some brutal side effects causing hallucinations and seizures. This is also now illegal, but it's easily accessible.

- Fentanyl: is an opiate that is more potent than heroin and morphine and used for severe pain or injury. When

  abused to obtain an elated high, the chance for overdose is high as is addiction. It can sometimes be mixed with cocaine or other stimulants. It's some crazy stuff.

- Bath Salts: a synthetic powder that typically has amphetamine components that brings on a high with a feeling of invincibility that's scary. There have been cases where hallucinations occur and individuals have literally eaten the faces of another human. This is legit scary crap.

- N-Bomb: a hallucinogen that is derived from mescaline sort of mimics the effects of LSD it typically is ingested in "tabs" that are sheets of paper or like stamps as well as in powder or spray form. Hallucinations can take place with trips that can cause kidney damage and can evoke feelings of psychosis.

- Sizzurp: mixing of cough syrup (with codeine) along with jolly ranchers or soda that gives a quick high, but can be brutal on the internal organs. It's a quick, inexpensive high.

- Ketamine: used as an anesthetic for both humans and animals it goes by Special K or Cat. It typically comes in powder form that can bring on hallucinations or feelings that are dream-like. It has been used to sedate victims slipped into drinks where they can them be sexually victimized without recalling what occurred due to it impairing memory.

There will always be revolving trends and making an effort to keep up with what they're called can be near impossible. My point being, don't allow yourself to become overwhelmed in feeling ill prepared for all that's out there. Do your utmost, ask questions, spend some time online and dialogue with family members. As adults, we need to know what's out there, but it should also not be an eyebrow -raising event when chatting about drugs comes into dinner time discussion. Knowledge and dialogue are empowering.

Knowledge is power. Learn about what's out there and know that what you don't know can hurt you. The vast majority of our culture has been affected by addiction. It may be a distant friend, co-worker or someone living under the same roof. It may be you.

When addiction is in force the individual is not a bad person, he or she is just making poor decisions that have the potential to do a whole lot of damage. Seeking support and forms of positive encouragement is important. Don't keep your eyes closed. Don't hold your breath and cross your fingers hoping time will make it go away. Help is out there. Taking that first step is scary, but it has the ability to be life altering. Don't go at it by yourself.

A fundamental principal of the twelve step program (A.A., N.A., etc.) is the serenity prayer. I believe that it's pretty powerful.

God grant me the serenity
To accept the things I cannot change;
Courage to change the things I can;
And wisdom to know the difference.
Living one day at a time;
Enjoying one moment at a time;
Accepting hardships as the pathway to peace;
Taking, as He did, this sinful world
As it is, not as I would have it;
Trusting that He will make all things right
If I surrender to His Will;
So that I may be reasonably happy in this life
And supremely happy with Him
Forever and ever in the next.
Amen.

Everyday is a gift. Addiction must be approached with as much support, consistency and faith as possible. Please seek out help and know that you're not alone.

Thus Saith The Drug Lady…

Life is a journey. Your experience is your own and no one on the planet can replicate you. In the Bible we are described as *"fearfully and wonderfully made."* I'm in awe of the complexity of our minds and intricacies of our bodies to function as they do. It is mind boggling what is involved in who we become from conception to death. It's crazy mind spinning stuff.

We are not meant to take on this journey alone. Sometimes the road can be daunting, disheartening and truly brutal. Each of us can have a voice not only for ourselves, but for those who may feel broken and down trodden. There is power in believing in your abilities. There is resilience found when we lift each other up and speak encouragement with our lips and resonate compassion with our actions. I find peace and confidence in what lies beyond this life in my faith in Jesus Christ. It's pretty sweet knowing I don't have to throw the weight of the world on my shoulders when He has my back and provides the purest form of love and sacrifice that has ever been given. I can say without question, God is my refuge and strength in a world that can be daunting and a life that is but a vapor. You don't have do life alone. How rad is that? John 3:16 and Hebrews 11:1 are two verses that have given me a heap of hope.

As onions, laundry washers and all around every day people life goes by quickly. How we live and the outlook we choose to take can have a huge bearing on its quality. Take life by the horns, don't allow your past to dictate your future and know that each day is a gift. Rock out life! Live with open arms and a receptive heart.

Peace, love and goodness.

72068403R00081

Made in the USA
Columbia, SC
14 June 2017